THE NEWS
AND HOW TO
UNDERSTAND IT

In spite of the newspapers
In spite of the magazines
In spite of the radio

BY QUINCY HOWE

GREENWOOD PRESS, PUBLISHERS
NEW YORK   1968

To

Eleanor and Elliott Sanger

TABLE OF CONTENTS

☆ ☆ ★ ☆ ☆

FOREWORD

☆ ☆ ☆ ☆ ☆

THIS IS A "how to" book about the news. It tells no inside story. It proposes no crusade. It has just one purpose—to show how you can get more pleasure and profit from following the news.

I am not myself a newspaperman and never have been. For the past eighteen years my main vocation and avocation have been to interpret world news. From 1922 to 1928 I worked on the staff of The Living Age and from 1929 to 1935 I served as its editor. I have written three books on world affairs and, since August, 1939, have been commenting on current news three times a week over Station WOXR in New York.

Most of this book deals with the raw material of the news and where it comes from. I have not attempted to cover all the newspapers, magazines, and radio stations or all the people from whom we get our news. I have confined myself to those news sources and news channels that reach the entire country. This means, specifically, the press associations and the people who write for them, the chief syndicates and the chief syndicate writers, a few of the more popular general magazines, and the radio networks.

And I have tried to explain all these organizations and the people who work for them in terms of their functions under present conditions, not in terms of what they might do under different circumstances.

Most books about the news approach the subject in a serious mood. Most "how to" books in any field offer little in the way of entertainment. Writing a "how to" book about the news, especially at this juncture of world history, therefore seemed about as dismal a job as anyone could tackle. But my learned colleague, J. A. Goodman, had an inspiration. I had expected to reprint a lot of old news stories, columns, editorials, radio scripts, and magazine articles to illustrate my various points. Mr. Goodman, however, suggested that I lay aside the scissors and paste and try my hand at parody. Therefore I have gone in for almost no quotation at all, but have written a number of short, satirical versions of some of the news features that I discuss. My underlying purpose, however, remains serious. It is to show how the people who report and interpret our news got the way they are.

I have received help from experts all along the line, but they prefer to remain anonymous because they want to stay on speaking terms with the people and organizations covered here. Myself, I can only hope that everything in this book is taken in exactly the spirit it was written.

Q. H.

September, 1940
New York City

☆ ☆ ☆ ☆ ☆

THE NEWS
AND HOW TO
UNDERSTAND IT

☆ ☆ ☆ ☆ ☆

☆ 1 ☆

WHAT'S NEWS?

☆ ☆ ☆ ☆ ☆

IF YOU SPEND fifteen minutes six days a week reading the daily papers, you are reading well over a million words a year. Another half-hour on the Sunday paper adds another half-million words to your annual total. If you average half an hour a week on magazines, that means half a million more. And if you listen to news broadcasts fifteen minutes a day, you hear almost a million words a year through that medium.

Where do these millions of words come from? What effect are they supposed to have on you? How can you get the most from them? Not only does the news itself affect our daily lives; the reports we get of that news determine our attitude toward the world around us. Many of our private thoughts and personal opinions, many of our secret hopes and intimate fears can be traced back to the publishers of newspapers and to the people who write for them, to the owners of radio stations, to the people who talk over the radio, even to the sponsors of radio programs. In consequence, we are more influenced by the way some event is interpreted than we are by the event itself.

Factual reporting of actual events forms only a tiny proportion of our national and foreign news. Most of it consists of interpretation. Our newspaper reporters and columnists, our radio newscasters and commentators devote much more time to explaining what the news means than they do to a recital of the bare facts. Often, in fact, it does not require more than a column of type or a five-minute broadcast to cover all the significant news of the day.

Some of the most important news already appears in highly condensed, even tabular, form. For instance, tucked away in the corner of your paper you will find the daily report of the United States Coast and Geodetic Survey. This report gives the hours of sunrise and sunset, the hours of high and low tide, and the dates when the moon goes into its next phases. Let us suppose, however, that for just one day this report became the basis for the standard type of news story or news comment. How would it read? The Associated Press, largest and oldest of our news-gathering agencies, would be likely to handle the material this way:

NEW YORK, August 3 (Associated Press)—John Smith, 38, of 27 Upland Road, Brooklyn, who has worked with the United States Coast and Geodetic Survey for the past fifteen years, issued a formal news release today stating that the sun will rise tomorrow morning at 5:54 A.M. and will set at 8:10 P.M. High water, Mr. Smith's release continued, can be expected at 8:06 A.M. and at 8:19 P.M., while low water will occur at 2:10 A.M. and at 2:13 P.M. The news release further stated that the moon will enter its first quarter on August 10 and that a full moon can be expected on August 17. Similar forecasts by Mr. Smith have proved reliable on previous occasions.

The more enterprising United Press, which prides itself on its speed and which permits its correspondents to offer some interpretation of the news, would probably handle the story this way:

NEW YORK, August 2 (United Press)—In the first exclusive interview that your correspondent has been granted since he talked with Stalin in the Kremlin, I was received today at the Brooklyn residence of Mrs. John Smith, whose husband has spent the past fifteen years in the service of the United States Coast and Geodetic Survey. Mrs. Smith, indignant at New Deal bureaucracy and wearing a faded Landon sunflower as well as a Willkie button, showed me confidential documents that her husband is preparing to release tomorrow. As a believer in free speech and a free press, Mrs. Smith said she felt this information should be made available at once to the people of America who have been lulled by the Roosevelt Administration into a sense of false security. But in view of the critical state of America's defenses and the increased activities of Fifth Columnists, the contents of Mrs. Smith's documents are being withheld for the moment and turned over

5

*to the Republican National Committee. All that can be
safely revealed to the general public is that Mr. Smith anticipates a full moon on the night of August 17.*

International News Service, a Hearst subsidiary, would
not only do its best to beat its two rivals; it would uncover
a story which they both had missed. Here, then, is the way
the same assignment might conceivably be handled by
H. R. Knickerbocker, ace correspondent of the INS organization:

SOMEWHERE IN AMERICA, *August 1 (INS)—Hitler is here.
I have seen a legion of brown-shirt parachute troops invade the heart of a peaceful American community close to
one of our large urban centers. In scoring this sensational
scoop I descended by parachute myself and I, too, wore a
brown shirt as well as a sun helmet, whipcord riding
breeches, spiral puttees, Sam Browne belt, field glasses, and
a set of earphones attached to a midget short-wave radio
receiving set concealed in my hip pocket. Leaping from
the wing of a specially chartered transport plane I landed
in the back yard of the secret hide-out of the German Ges-
tapo's number-one operator who, under the name of John
Smith, has insinuated himself into a key government department. Shortly after I had made my landing and had
disentangled myself from my parachute, I saw a troop of
about twenty-five or thirty small men wearing brown shirts
and shouting in falsetto voices. The moment I landed,*

they dashed around a corner and deployed in a stretch of wooded country where they soon vanished from sight. Their Gruppenführer (group leader) was tall and dark and all of them carried long thin weapons that looked at a distance like harmless sticks but that were actually deadly Feuerwerfen (flame throwers) that spray liquid fire or poison gas.

The back door of the "Smith" residence stood open, but suspecting that it might be guarded by an invisible death ray, I entered the house through the kitchen window, forcing the latch with my pocketknife. On the table of the living room I found several yellow sheets of paper with figures scribbled on them. These I quickly photographed with my miniature camera, leaving them, however, in their original positions. Apparently the figures dealt with the hours of sunrise and sunset, the times of the tides, and the phases of the moon, but it was instantly clear to the eye of a trained journalist that they actually concealed a secret code. I have therefore turned them over to the Federal Bureau of Investigation.

I was on the point of continuing my search to the upper stories when I saw a Boy Scout walking up the front path toward the house. As I turned to flee I could not help noticing a remarkable resemblance between him and the storm troopers I had observed when I made my own parachute landing. But just as Hitler disguised his soldiers in Dutch uniforms during the conquest of Holland, so in the conquest of America, which has now begun, he is disguis-

ing them as Boy Scouts. Which gives me an idea for tomorrow's assignment: disguise myself as an ordinary newspaperman with felt hat, business suit, and portable typewriter. It ought to be sensational. Or at least terrific.

It is a dull day indeed that does not give Dorothy Thompson an excuse for writing one of her open letters to Congress, and these are some of the changes she might ring on our sun, moon, and tide story:

An Open Letter to the Congress of the United States

GENTLEMEN: *Fill your fountain pens. Sharpen your pencils. Get out your little red notebooks. All set? Now take dictation.*

America must act! America must act!! Do you hear me? AMERICA MUST ACT!!! For if we do not act, gentlemen, do you realize that we face the same fate as Manchuria, Ethiopia, Austria, Spain, China, Czechoslovakia, Lithuania, Latvia, Esthonia, Finland, Denmark, Norway, Sweden, Holland, Belgium, France, Rumania, England? Do you realize this, gentlemen? Don't interrupt. The answer is no. And why do we face this fate? Because our government devotes all its energies to maintaining such antiquated enterprises as the United States Coast and Geodetic Survey. Can you imagine it? The United States Coast and Geodetic Survey! Did you ever hear of anything so ridiculous? What does it mean? What does it do?

Frankly, I don't know and I don't care. But what I do know is that the money now being spent on superfluous services of this kind should be spent on toughening the fiber of the younger generation.

Why? Because the United States must at once DE-CLARE WAR ON THE ENTIRE WORLD. Germany, Japan, Russia, and Italy now control three large continents with a total population of one and a half billion people. Do not correct me if I am wrong. My research assistant will have the right figure in later editions. And here is the peril that faces this country. Hitler is rapidly killing off all the people living under German domination. Stalin, Mussolini, and the Mikado are also doing their best to exterminate all human life in their spheres of influence. Unless America quickly does its share, the rest of the world will therefore kill itself off and we shall be left—alone.

Walter Winchell would present the same material in some such fashion as this:

The Winchell Column Against the Fifth Column. Although Ratzi agents will try to tell you different, the sun will rise tomorrow yawning at 4:54—5:54 to you, you dope, Daylight Saving Time (haw!). * * * It will also be high water at H-ll Gate Bridge five hours later. . . . Aside to J. Edgar Hoover's G-Men: What is this high water trying to cover up? . . . And to Mr. and Mrs. America: When the sun is still shining on the Stars and Stripes across San

Francisco Bay, it is midnight in Moscow already and the Communazis are readying another blast against Mrs. Winchell's little boy Walter whose blood is bright red, whose spirit is pure white, and whose courage is true blue. So I'm just a flag-waving hysteric??? FOOEY!

Walter Lippmann would bring quite a different, but similarly personalized, style to bear:

In these times that try men's souls, America has a rendezvous with destiny. Men must act, but action without thought is as futile as thought without action. The wise man thinks before he acts, acts after he thinks. The fool acts before he thinks, thinks after he acts. If America is to keep her rendezvous with destiny we must think first and act afterward.

But before we can think or act, we must have facts on which to base our thoughts and actions. This morning's paper, for example, brings us the reports of the United States Coast and Geodetic Survey. Yet can a conscientious reader give these reports full credence? Can we be sure that a negligent compositor, safely protected from dismissal by his corrupt and inefficient trade union, has not made a mistake which, in turn, the proofreader, a member of the Newspaper Guild, has failed to detect? Or again, is it not possible that the agents of certain foreign powers—I exclude, of course, our British cousins from this category—may have insinuated themselves into our government serv-

10

:es and are hampering our defense program by giving out
ilse information? An inaccurate schedule of tide tables,
or example, might levy a grievous toll on our shipping,
ausing our loyal officers to run their craft on rocks, reefs,
nud flats, and the half-submerged wrecks of American
'essels, scuttled by their mutinous CIO crews. In short,
:he American newspaper reader faces perils as menacing in
:heir way as any of the terrors of the deep. Only unceasing
vigilance will enable us to steer our ship of state through
the troubled waters that lie ahead.

These six imaginary items of news and news interpretation show how differently our three chief news-gathering
agencies and three of our most popular columnists would
handle the same story. They also illustrate a point I made
at the outset, a point that might be defined as follows:
nine words out of every ten that we read in the newspapers give us opinions, not facts; interpretation, not
news.

There are two reasons for this state of affairs. In the
first place, facts and news are hard to come by; in the second place, opinion and interpretation make better reading. In other words, our present newspaper diet gives as
much satisfaction to the producers as it does to the con-
sumers. Moreover, a newspaper that tried to reverse the
present ten-to-one proportion would find it hard sledding.

At this point a word of definition is in order. When I
speak of "news" I have in mind such events as the

Munich Conference of 1938, the Nazi-Soviet Pact of 1939, the capitulation of France in 1940. The bare reports of these three occurrences—the official documents, the statements made by the chief participants, the descriptions of the actual ceremonies—filled relatively little space. Even straight action stories, like the British evacuation of Dunkirk, the German invasion of Norway, the Russian bombardment of the Mannerheim Line, required considerable interpretation and explanation.

The newspapers and radio might, of course, dig up more facts than they do. But the biggest news stories are not "dug up"; they just happen in God's good time. And it is these big news stories that are the main concern of most correspondents and commentators. As for the public, what it wants and needs is not more Munich Conferences, not more evacuations of Dunkirk. What it wants and needs is more and better interpretation.

This applies especially to world news and leads to still another word of explanation. Actually, newspapers and radio stations perform three distinct services. One of these services is to gather and disseminate the news—local news, national news, foreign news. And it is with national and foreign news that this book is exclusively concerned. But the two other services that our newspapers and radio stations perform should be mentioned in passing. One of these services is to provide diversion; the other is to provide practical, as distinct from general, information. In the case of a newspaper, diversion means comics, puzzles, society

12

news, and sports. In the case of radio, diversion means music, sporting events, variety acts, and the like. In the case of a newspaper, practical information means weather reports, stock listings, radio schedules, and women's features. In the case of radio, practical information includes educational programs, weather and crop reports, and household hints. These aspects of "the news" do not, however, come into the scope of this particular book. Here I am concerned only with world news and its interpretation.

And our newspapers and radio have two main functions in connection with world news. One function is to gather the news and the other function is to interpret it. Almost always, of course, the newspapers and radio telescope the two functions. Even the most factual type of news reporting contains some interpretation; even the most opinionated columnist or radio commentator provides some facts. It is my purpose in this book to break down this balanced diet of fact and opinion and show how it can give you more nourishment. This is not a technical study of how newspaper stories, newspaper columns, or radio broadcasts are put together. Neither is it an expose. I am concerned solely with the actual material now available, and with how you can use that material most effectively.

I shall begin by discussing newspapers, because most of our news—even most of the news we get over the radio— comes from newspaper sources. I shall then devote two chapters to books and magazines and a couple of chapters to radio. Moreover, in order to illustrate the points I shall want to make, and to provide a touch of (perhaps) comic relief, I shall put at the end of some of the chapters several more satires like those with which this chapter opened.

But first of all, let us look at this whole question of understanding the news from your point of view. Let us try to see it through the eyes of the ultimate consumer.

14

☆ 2 ☆

KNOW YOURSELF

☆ ☆ ☆ ☆ ☆

BEFORE YOU can understand the news you must understand two aspects of yourself. First, you must know what kind of reader or listener you are. Second, you must develop and frankly recognize some point of view of your own toward world affairs. For there isn't any right way or any wrong way to understand the news. There is only a right way for you and a wrong way for you.

Some people want to understand the news for bread-and-butter reasons. They seek some kind of profit from their newspaper reading and radio listening. Other people want to understand the news for sheer self-satisfaction. They get pleasure, or at any rate stimulation, from reading and listening to the news. Finally, there are the people who want to understand the news in order to escape from some personal difficulty. Most of us, of course, follow the news for a combination of all three reasons. We must therefore decide how much profit, how much pleasure, and how much escape we can find in the news, and proceed accordingly.

If you follow the news primarily in order to understand

how it may affect you personally, your main problem is one of time. This means that you must know what newspapers and magazines you need not read, what radio programs you need not listen to. And in the newspapers you do read, you must concentrate on skimming the headlines—all of them—but you seldom need to read the complete text of any news story. Budget the time you spend following the news, and you will not only have more time left for other pursuits; you will actually achieve a better grasp of world affairs.

For instance, if you read the papers primarily for profit and rather grudge the time they take, read only one paper a day—preferably a morning edition. Other things being equal, you will find it gives you a much more complete news coverage. This is because the news from Europe comes pouring across the cables during the day, and usually peters out by seven o'clock, New York time, when it is midnight over there. Washington news, however, keeps coming in all evening. The afternoon and evening papers give you flashes of this news as it arrives, but it takes most of the evening to co-ordinate and interpret everything that has happened. So why not wait until morning and get the complete news, properly organized?

The answer is that you may require some of the news in the evening paper that same evening—the complete Stock Exchange listings, for instance. Or again, your social duties may virtually compel you to keep posted on the events of the day. Or you may live in the Chicago area where the

16

Chicago Daily News, an evening paper, maintains a foreign service so far superior to the morning *Tribune's* that you cannot afford to miss it. What you will probably want to do is read one paper for one thing, another for another. In New York, for instance, the columnists in the *World-Telegram* strike a nice balance with the news dispatches in the morning *Times.* The busy reader can skip the *World-Telegram's* news columns, and there aren't many columnists in the *Times* anyway.

The busy reader, the reader for profit, can pretty well dispense with the radio. It takes two or three times as long to listen to a news broadcast as it does to read the same material yourself—and you cannot skip parts of a broadcast; you must listen to the whole thing. Moreover, the straight news broadcast gives a condensed version of the same news dispatches you get in your newspaper, for the same news agencies—the Associated Press, the United Press, and the International News Service—provide the information. Only if you are out of reach of a newspaper, or want to get the highlights of the news a few hours before it appears in the press, will you find it worth while to bother with news broadcasts.

Most of the commentators, except Swing and Kaltenborn, do more summarizing than interpreting; Elmer Davis, however, performs a miracle of condensation in five minutes each evening. It is no accident that these three men have gained new listeners more rapidly than any of their colleagues. The only other radio feature that repays regular listening is the Columbia Broadcasting System's roundup of the foreign capitals. If you live beyond the reach of a good metropolitan daily paper, you might subscribe to *Time* or *Newsweek* and confine your newspaper reading to local items and special features. *Time* and *Newsweek* have attracted more than a million readers between them because the daily papers published in many of our larger cities—notably Boston, Pittsburgh, and Los Angeles—do such a sloppy job of news coverage. But for my money, wherever I lived, I'd want to see *The New York Times*, daily and Sunday, and I believe I'd still be getting more news in less time than I could find anywhere else.

I introduce the personal equation because this matter of following the news is first and foremost a personal affair. The recommendations listed so far are put forward merely as suggestions, not as requirements. It is essential for the individual to make the final decision, and, since it is an individual matter, consult your own tastes, needs, and prejudices and nobody else's. If, for instance, you grudge the time you spend following the news, your main problem is to organize yourself. On the other hand, if you get a real kick out of reading the newspapers and listening to the radio, take the rough suggestions I have given and build from there. You know what you like—simply indulge yourself.

Just as the person who grudges the time it takes to follow the news should deliberately cut all the corners he can, so the person who enjoys following the news should just as deliberately invite his soul. If you know what you like, that means you have some individual philosophy or point of view around which you should be able to organize your reading and listening. Your chief task is to recognize the reality of your own prejudices and proceed accordingly. To minister, quite deliberately, to these prejudices is the beginning of wisdom. You may be objective—even neutral—in your attitude toward Hitler or Churchill, Roosevelt or Stalin. You are not, however, either neutral or objective in your attitude toward yourself and toward your own powers of judgment. None of us is. We may be able to stomach a lot of unpleasant items in the news, but there is one thing none of us can tolerate, especially those of us who spend a good deal of time following the news, and that is the possibility that our own estimate of this news may be cockeyed. This does not mean that you should cling, doggedly, to a rigid set of convictions. It means only that you recognize your convictions, allow for them, and understand them, because if you do not understand them you will not understand anything else.

As a matter of fact, if you enjoy trying to understand the news, you are already doing this, consciously or otherwise. It is only if you are trying to escape from your own troubles by losing yourself in the larger troubles of the larger world that you may come to grief. For, if you follow the news for escapist reasons, the more papers you read and the more broadcasts you listen to, the worse you will feel. You may not, of course, feel as bad as if you were brooding about yourself, but the spectacle the world presents today does not exactly encourage serenity in the minds of newspaper readers or radio listeners.

Here is a recent case history. In June, 1940, a gathering of psychiatrists in New York heard an expert in the field read a paper stating that the war had led to an alarming increase in nervous breakdowns. It is generally assumed that the war caused the breakdowns, but there are psychologists who argue that the war merely offered a convenient outlet for neurotics who were headed for trouble anyway. Whether the war accelerated the breakdowns or whether it acted as a tonic by taking the victims' minds off their own troubles is a question for the experts.

If you follow the news in order to get away from yourself, you must organize some attitude of your own toward the world around you. I do not refer here to a personal philosophy. On the contrary. It is an impersonal point of view that I am recommending. Even a lot of well-balanced people who have their personal lives under complete control do not know what to think about the world outside. And in like manner, it is quite possible for a neurotic to compensate for his lack of a personal philosophy by developing a political, an economic, or a social philosophy which can be applied to the news of the day. Indeed, the neurotic more often than not can rout the nonneurotic in a discussion of Marxism, the gold standard, or the moral case for war.

Without expounding my own views, let me suggest a

few angles from which you can drill your news sources with some expectation of striking oil. And I shall do this by raising some of the questions you might ask yourself— whether you are a neurotic or a nonneurotic—as you read or listen to the news. For instance:

Does the war in Europe seem to you primarily a war of rival empires, like the last one, or is it a kind of social revolution? Do you think the Soviet Union is a totalitarian dictatorship like Nazi Germany or does it seem to you to have a basically different character? What is your attitude toward Great Britain? Is it primarily a world empire or is it primarily a democracy? And as for our own relation to the rest of the world, should we strive for complete isolation, should we undertake the defense of the Western Hemisphere, or should we intervene in the Far East and Europe as well?

Only a fool will give categorical answers to these questions. Only a fool has a copper-riveted philosophy, adequate to all emergencies. But it is equally foolish not to have any opinions at all, not to have even the vaguest outlines of a philosophy. The person who knows all the answers does not need to follow the news; he understands it all anyway. The person who has no opinions may try to follow the news, but he will wind up in the psychiatric ward because he will believe everything he reads and hears. What I am suggesting here is an approach, a direction. For, if you have a general approach, if you know the crucial questions you want answered, you will get a lot more out of what you read and hear. Also, if you have some prejudices, you will not waste your time and wear out your nerves considering points of view with which you do not agree.

One final word of summary and conclusion. All of us seek three things in the news—profit, pleasure, and escape. None of us reads the news for just one or even two of these things. All of us are after all three of them. It is only in our emphasis that we differ. To understand the news, all of us must therefore organize ourselves in three directions. First, we must organize our underlying beliefs and cultivate at least a few prejudices and convictions. With all there is going on in the world, this should not be too difficult a job. Then, having organized our prejudices, we must deliberately minister to those prejudices in the news we read or listen to over the radio. One person may like to indulge his prejudices; another may prefer to rub them the wrong way. It is simply a question of taste. Finally, when we have organized and recognized our prejudices, we can begin to work out a definite schedule. The succeeding chapters will inspect the raw material now available to newspaper and magazine readers and to radio listeners in all parts of the country. The concluding chapter will offer specific recommendations.

☆ 3 ☆

PRESS ASSOCIATIONS AND THE PRESS

☆ ☆ ☆ ☆ ☆

THE LAST CHAPTER touched on three functions that the news performs in your daily life. Moreover, it was my contention that you cannot understand the news unless you first understand that its triple function is to yield profit, pleasure, and escape. We now come to the channels through which we get our news, and here, too, we must raise the same kind of realistic questions. What is the purpose, what is the function of the press association that gathers so much of our news, and what is the purpose, what is the function of the newspapers that print this news?

Three organizations gather most of the news you read in your newspaper and hear over the radio. The Associated Press, largest and oldest of our news-gathering agencies, is a membership organization, owned and co-operatively controlled by 1437 American newspaper publishers. The United Press, a profit-making subsidiary of the Scripps-Howard enterprises, has been offering the Associated Press increasingly severe competition, especially during the past ten years. It is not a membership organization, but sells its service at a price to all comers. International News Service, a Hearst subsidiary, operates exactly like the United Press, but where the Associated Press has always specialized in accuracy and the United Press in speed, International News Service has specialized in sensations.

As a nonprofit organization, the Associated Press is primarily interested in giving its restricted membership better service than they can get anywhere else. The cost of this service is based on the literate population in the area that each member paper serves. When there are two or more Associated Press newspapers in one area, they divide the cost equally. To receive Associated Press service a newspaper must be elected into the association by the other Associated Press newspapers in its district or else purchase a local paper that already has an Associated Press franchise. In the larger cities it is virtually impossible to get Associated Press service without buying up an old paper first, because one blackball by any local paper can keep out competition.

With 1437 newspapers contributing to its support, all of them jealous of the privileges and profits of membership, the Associated Press offers the most extensive news coverage available in this country or anywhere else. Until recent years, the Associated Press also offered the dullest news that human ingenuity could produce. Its thousands of reporters were forbidden to speculate about the news, to interpret it, to circulate rumors. They were instructed to confine themselves to the facts, and any correspondent

24

who tried to put color or personality into his writing got the boot. But the competition of rival news agencies has produced a change. Especially in its coverage of the present war, the Associated Press has relaxed some of its restrictions. It still keeps its correspondents as anonymous as possible, but it has done its share in spreading sensation for sensation's sake.

There are two reasons for this change of policy. In the first place, sensations sell papers, and the competition of the other news services has forced the Associated Press to lay more emphasis on sensation than it once did. In the second place, the people who supply the news often want its sensational aspects emphasized. Especially is this true in a nation at war. There the authorities have no objection to dramatic reporting. What they fear is not drama in the news, but unpleasant facts or rumors. Censorship and propaganda operate on a larger scale than ever before. The results stare you in the face every time you pick up a newspaper. Today we have the most efficient technical equipment to gather news and the most competent correspondents to write it. Yet because of—not in spite of—all this technical excellence, we have received far more misinformation about the Second World War, we know far less about what has really been happening in Europe since September, 1939, than we did during the corresponding period of the last war.

The entire blame for this state of affairs cannot be laid at the door of the Associated Press or any other news agency. The blame lies partly with the American public's craving for sensation and partly with the eagerness of our news sources at home and abroad to indulge this craving. Where the Associated Press and other news agencies can be justly criticized is in their interpretation of the news they get. Competition between rival newspapers, and competition between rival news agencies, have put a premium on headlines, especially in a period of war. Therefore, the Associated Press and its two competitors play up for all they are worth the headline possibilities in any given story and urge their correspondents to write with the headlines always in mind.

Within these limitations—the limitations of the news itself and the limitations of competition—Associated Press policy reflects the interests of the membership. In the spring of 1940, 75 per cent of the newspapers using Associated Press service opposed the New Deal. Yet only three of the eighteen directors of the Associated Press call their papers Republican or independent Republican. Seven of them call themselves Democratic or independent Democratic, and eight call themselves independent. The Democrats, however, include Paul Bellamy, editor of the pro-Willkie *Cleveland Plain Dealer*, and the independents include Colonel Robert R. McCormick, publisher of the *Chicago Tribune*, the most reactionary big newspaper in the country.

This does not mean that the Associated Press is a puppet organization, controlled by "outside interests" or manipulated from behind the scenes. Actually, it is chartered as a club, not as a corporation, and newspapermen call it "the Rod and Gun Club." When the liberal crusader, Oswald Garrison Villard, served as director of the Associated Press, he complained that it was constitutionally incapable of doing justice to the underdog. An article on the Associated Press in the February, 1937, issue of *Fortune* stated, "In labor policy, the AP has been steadily reactionary." After all, the big newspaper proprietors have substantially the same interests and the same point of view as any other entrenched minority. They have a large stake in things as they are; they employ labor; most of them have not yet awakened to the fact that liberal policies may pay bigger dividends than conservative ones. More of them should take to heart the career of Captain Joseph Patterson, proprietor of the *Daily News* of New York. This ex-Socialist has built up the biggest circulation in the United States by ministering to the tastes and prejudices of his readers. He quickly signed a contract with the American Newspaper Guild; he has steadily supported the New Deal; he has made a mint of money.

The kind of conservatism that characterizes the Associated Press—and the kind that has done it the most harm —is neither a political nor an economic conservatism. It is an organizational conservatism. Every big enterprise finds itself sooner or later in this position, and the Associated Press is no exception. But there is another side of the picture. The wide coverage of the Associated Press gives

27

its reporters the inside track to almost all the biggest news stories. The Associated Press also has exclusive exchange arrangements with all the official and semiofficial news agencies abroad. These agencies, of course, hand out only what the government wants distributed, but in the kingdom of the blind, the one-eyed man is king. Finally, the Associated Press has the greatest wire-photo service in the world. This means that Associated Press newspapers get more and better pictures sooner than their competitors— a vital matter in building circulation.

Just as the Associated Press has enlivened its style in recent years, so its chief competitor, the United Press, has grown so fast that it is rapidly acquiring the curse of bigness which has hampered AP efficiency in the past. In other words, the two chief American news agencies are getting more and more alike. The third, International News Service, has also grown, but in recent years it has not kept pace with its rivals. A few figures will clarify the picture at this point.

The Associated Press spends $11,000,000 a year collecting news. It leases 300,000 miles of telegraph wire in the United States alone. It releases 200,000 words of news a day to its 1437 members. The United Press spends $8,-000,000 a year and leases 150,000 miles of wire in the United States. It sends out 150,000 words a day to 975 American newspapers and to more than 300 foreign newspapers, most of them in Latin America. The outbreak of the war cost the United Press most of its 200 European newspapers. International News Service leases 170,000 miles of wire and sends 150,000 words a day to 700 newspapers.

The Associated Press was founded in 1847; it has gone through several reorganizations, the last one in 1927. The United Press was founded in 1907 by the late E. W. Scripps, a great newspaper crusader who resented the idea of a news monopoly and insisted that news be sold for cash to all comers. A year after Scripps launched the United Press, Hearst launched the International News Service, also a frankly commercial news-gathering agency. Today, the Scripps-Howard interests own the United Press, while International News Service has become the subsidiary of still another Hearst subsidiary—King Features.

What are the distinguishing features of the United Press service? What can you expect to find in a United Press dispatch that you will not find in an Associated Press dispatch? The United Press specializes in scoops, style, interpretation, and personality. Associated Press dispatches rarely carry the names of their authors; United Press dispatches almost always do. This policy has occasionally got the United Press into hot water, the most sensational incident being the premature armistice report cabled from France to the United States on November 7, 1918, by Roy Howard, now the dominating figure in the Scripps-Howard chain and the United Press. Day in, day out, however, the United Press tries to beat the Associated Press and frequently does get its reports in first. United Press dispatches also offer more interpretation than the Associated Press.

The United Press is almost as free of outside control as the Associated Press. It is owned by the E. W. Scripps Company of Cincinnati. This holding company also controls the eighteen Scripps-Howard papers, a syndicate bureau known as the Newspaper Enterprise Association, and numerous other press services. All seven of the Scripps directors have come up through the ranks of the newspaper business or else belong to the Scripps or the Howard families. The only outside money in the Scripps-Howard empire takes the form of a bond issue of $8,500,000 floated in 1928 through several banks with Morgan and Van Sweringen connections. But Wall Street and Morgan influence have played no discernible part in shaping Scripps-Howard policy. For one thing, the Scripps-Howard enterprises make too much money to have to take orders from anybody. For another, it didn't require any outside pressure to persuade Roy Howard to shift the support he gave Roosevelt in 1936 to Willkie in 1940. There was never a more honest conversion.

The Scripps-Howard newspaper chain, like the Hearst newspaper chain, originated in California, for that was where Mr. Scripps got his start in the newspaper business. Roy Howard, a whole generation younger than his partner, worked his way to the top and now makes his headquarters in New York, though he still keeps enough Ohio connections to remain somewhat independent of Wall Street. While Hearst's dwindling influence does not cut much ice outside California, Roy Howard's is concentrated in the Middle West. Howard himself is a dapper little man whose loud shirts and suits bespeak an energetic personality. He takes little active part in the day to day management of the United Press; that is in the hands of a whole hierarchy of officials. But through his control of the Scripps-Howard holding company, Roy Howard remains the real power behind the throne. Because the United Press foreign correspondents cannot always afford to keep up with the local Joneses, Howard keeps dashing all over the world picking up interviews himself and functioning as a member of the working press—his greatest joy.

Hugh Baillie, president of the United Press, has also spent his whole life in the newspaper business. Born in Brooklyn fifty years ago, he attended the University of Southern California and went to work on a Los Angeles newspaper in 1910. Between 1915 and 1920 he served as manager of the United Press bureaus in half a dozen different American cities, including Washington and New York, and then became general news manager of the organization. He has held executive jobs ever since and has been president of the United Press since 1935. And, true to newspaper tradition, he married a newspaperwoman.

The United Press owes most of its success to superior writing, more personal interpretation, and greater speed. The Associated Press finally had to pay the younger organization the compliment of imitation, and today these two great news agencies vie with each other for front-page stories that lend themselves to sensational headlines. But the United Press steers almost as clear of controversy as the Associated Press. Scripps-Howard policy is one thing; United Press policy is something else again. The Scripps-Howard newspapers supported Roosevelt in 1936; most subscribers to the United Press opposed him. But all the news services reported the campaign fully and with reasonable objectivity. Newspaper proprietors know that their readers hold varying points of view; therefore, in covering outstanding public officials, newspapers usually assign to each official a reporter who is reasonably sympathetic—personally if not politically. Thus, the Republican *New York Herald Tribune* had Ernest K. Lindley covering Mr. Roosevelt from the 1932 campaign on into his second term, during which period Mr. Lindley wrote two books boosting the New Deal. In like manner, the news services try to assign the right reporter to the right story.

Where much of the bias comes in is not in the text of the news dispatch, but in the way the individual newspaper presents the material it receives from the press associations. This bias may take the form of headlines, excisions, or position in the paper. Republican papers play up even the dullest Hoover speeches; New Deal papers play up Ickes. But the most successful papers, alert to reader interest, have found it wise not to load the dice too heavily. In sheer self-protection they present both sides of controversial issues.

The growing interest in news for the sake of news has

made the press associations prosper. No sooner did Scripps-Howard organize the United Press to compete with the Associated Press in 1907 than William Randolph Hearst launched the International News Service to compete with both. Alfred McClung Lee's *Daily Newspaper in America* quotes the following definition of Hearst-INS policy in the words of the organization itself: "Get the news. Get it first. Spare no expense. Make a great and continuous noise to attract readers; denounce crooked wealth and promise better conditions to the poor. Increase circulation." Although some Hearst and Scripps-Howard papers have Associated Press franchises and can therefore vote on Associated Press policy, neither Mr. Hearst nor Mr. Howard has ever exerted any measurable influence on the AP. Indeed, it may be doubted that they have ever tried.

Three distinguishing features have marked every enterprise associated with the name of Hearst. The first is sensationalism; the second is ruthlessness; the third is extraneous, crusading fervor. And it is Hearst's crusading fervor that has proved his undoing. Contrary to popular assumption, Hearst's yellow journalism and his ruthless pursuit of the news tended on the whole to raise American newspaper standards. He introduced many technical innovations; his writers enlivened the style of their competitors; when other newspapers did not deign to meet him on his own ground, they had to do a better job on theirs. Yet in spite of all the dust Hearst raised, his career as a whole can hardly be described as successful. Unable to float a $35,000,000 bond issue a few years ago, Hearst has had to borrow smaller sums on his personal, tangible assets, while his newspaper properties have become obligated to the Chase National Bank, the Metropolitan Life Insurance Company, and the Equitable Life. In short, Hearst is now under obligations to those same capitalists with the dollar signs on their vests whom his cartoonists used to satirize.

What caused the disintegration of the Hearst empire? Changing conditions played a part, but they do not tell the whole story. From his earliest days, Hearst has regarded newspapers as means toward an end rather than an end in themselves. He has interested himself in many reforms, many causes. Often he has reversed himself. A regular Democrat until the time of Woodrow Wilson, he first opposed and then supported our participation in the last war. During the twenties the Hearst papers backed Coolidge and Hoover, but shifted to Roosevelt in 1932. In 1936 Hearst rooted for Landon, but immediately after the election reverted briefly to Roosevelt again. Traditionally anti-British, he became in the early twenties the temporary advocate of an Anglo-American alliance to rule the world. At the start of his career, his attacks on entrenched wealth won him friends in the labor movement. Today organized labor regards him as public enemy number one.

But in addition to changing his mind on issues and changing his party loyalties from campaign to campaign and even from state to state, Hearst has never devoted him-

34

self entirely to becoming the great newspaper publisher he might have been. If he had not drained off so much energy fighting quixotic political battles, if he had chosen the path of Adolph S. Ochs, he might have achieved all his ambitions—in the newspaper field and out of it. Ochs always remained primarily a newspaper publisher who first made *The New York Times* a great newspaper and then used it to promote his pet causes. With Ochs it was the newspaper first and the cause afterward. But with Hearst it has always been the other way around. He has frittered away his energies running for public office, taking up a thousand and one causes, and turning his newspapers into so many three-ring circuses. His methods have always attracted attention, but his changing schemes, ambitions, and enthusiasms keep his newspapers in a constant turmoil.

Hearst has stood for so many different things at different times and places that it is impossible to say what he stands for today. With his own newspaper properties heavily mortgaged, he cannot operate as freely as he once did, and in the case of International News Service, the organization stands at two removes from Hearst himself. Technically, INS is a subsidiary of King Features, the Hearst syndicate which sells all sorts of features and writers to all sorts of newspapers. And since INS, like the other services sold by King Features, must please a great variety of clients, it does not contain much editorializing. Rather does it specialize in big names—Walter Winchell among the columnists, Robert Ripley among the cartoonists, Karl Von Wiegand and H. R. Knickerbocker among the foreign correspondents. These individuals express their own points of view, exploit their own personalities. Meanwhile, Hearst himself has become a columnist in his old age. He always wrote many of the editorials his newspapers carried, but he now produces a long, daily column, "In the News." This does not bear his signature but it goes out of its way to reveal its authorship by frequent references to the author's experiences which exactly coincide with the experiences of Hearst. Here, if anywhere, you will find what William Randolph Hearst really believes about the world we live in. For the rest, his newspapers and other services offer little but sensationalized dullness, yellow journalism turned respectable.

What conclusions can the newspaper reader draw about the three great press associations? Any press association has more facilities for covering the news than any independent newspaper or any individual correspondent. Any press-association dispatch is written primarily to give information to many different newspapers pursuing many different policies. The press associations must maintain a high level of accuracy. Two of them are competing against each other and against the Associated Press; the Associated Press is answerable only to its members. Competition thus forces the press associations to report the news as quickly and accurately as possible. Their enormous resources also enable them to cover the news in greater detail.

36

It often happens that only two or three correspondents are permitted to cover a given story. On such occasions the press associations naturally get the inside track. This does not mean that you should read every press-association dispatch before you read any other. It means that you will be better informed if you read a paper that subscribes to at least two of the three press services.

Although the United Press and International News Service offer more in the way of interpretation, the chief weakness of all the press associations is that they must try to be all things to all men. Also, because all of them belong in the field of "big business," they not only give the news as conservative a slant as the traffic will bear; they suffer from the organizational curse of bigness. Finally, competition has encouraged uniformity. The United Press, it is true, does not follow quite such a conservative direction as its two competitors, because the men who control it are not themselves so basically conservative as the big newspaper publishers who dominate the Associated Press or the banks and insurance companies to which the Hearst empire is now so heavily mortgaged. But the growth of the United Press has given it some of the stuffiness that used to be an AP monopoly, while the livelier methods of the UP and the INS have caused the Associated Press to relax some of its standards.

Competition for news stories is the lifeblood of the press associations. The agency that scores the most scoops, creates the most headlines, and attracts the most public attention, gets the most business. And there is just one place that business comes from: the newspapers that use press-association service.

The newspaper, on the other hand, has two principal sources of revenue. One quarter of the income of the average American newspaper comes from circulation—the sale of copies to readers. Three quarters of the income of the average American newspaper comes from advertising. Every newspaper in the United States costs more to produce—far more—than its readers pay for it. New York's new five-cent tabloid, *PM*, may prove that at least one paper in at least one city can operate without advertising, but it has not yet emerged from the experimental stage. "We are here to sell advertising," Roy Howard told a luncheon of the Denver Chamber of Commerce when he was boosting the local Scripps-Howard paper. And there was nothing in the least cynical about this statement. It described one of the elementary facts about the newspaper business.

But in order to sell advertising a newspaper must attract circulation—and this is where the press associations come in. Few American newspapers can themselves afford to gather the bulk of their out-of-town news. For most of their Washington news, for almost all their foreign news, most American newspapers depend on the press associations or else on syndicates that sell certain writers and news services. Nearly three hundred newspapers or news agencies maintain correspondents in Washington. Barely half a dozen American newspapers maintain bureaus of their own in the chief foreign capitals. It is only in the field of local news that a paper depends on the members of its own staff or on a local news-gathering agency.

But whereas the news associations draw all their revenue from the sale of their services, the newspapers depend on their advertisers for seventy-five cents in every dollar they receive. Bearing in mind, then, the importance of advertising revenue, you obviously cannot expect the average American newspaper to denounce the largest department store in town as a fire hazard or a sweatshop. Neither can you expect the average American newspaper to attack the whole social order under which it at least hopes to prosper. Newspapers also depend on the good will of their readers. That is why you will not find any newspaper of general circulation attacking any powerful minority such as the Roman Catholic Church.

To criticize a newspaper because it supports the system under which it operates, or because it strives to please its advertisers and readers, is to criticize a bee because it stings or a dog because it barks. That is the nature of the beast. The only legitimate criticism that can be made against a newspaper is that it does not do the job it has set out to do. You may not like that job; you may not like the setting in which the job is being done. That is your privilege. The problem here, however, is to understand your newspaper by understanding its function. Which is not to say that

39

your newspaper necessarily understands this function itself.

For instance, when 86 per cent of the newspapers in the United States supported Landon in 1936 and Roosevelt carried all but two states, the influence of the press seemed to have reached an all-time low. One of *Fortune's* polls showed more than 20 per cent of the cross section of the public who were interviewed expressing lack of confidence in their newspapers; other polls showed that more people trust what they hear over the radio than what they read in the press. But even admitting that America's newspaper publishers fell out of step with the times and failed to command much political influence, was this such an unprecedented state of affairs? In the British general election of 1929 only one daily newspaper in all the British Isles—the *Daily Herald,* with a circulation at that time of 300,000—supported the Labor Party, yet Labor won more seats than any other party in the House of Commons.

The truth is that the modern newspaper is not primarily concerned with exercising political leadership. The modern newspaper is primarily concerned with providing a service. Thus, getting out a newspaper involves constant compromise. A sensational newspaper will win readers and advertisers away from a dull newspaper until it steps on too many toes. A dependable newspaper will win readers and advertisers away from an inaccurate one until it puts its readers to sleep. But what really determines a newspaper's success is the all-around quality of its service.

This service, as I have already indicated, takes the form of news, diversion, and practical information, and different people prefer this service in different proportions and different forms. You do not, for instance, buy a tabloid to get the complete text of Nicholas Murray Butler's latest speech. Neither do you buy *The New York Times* for crossword puzzles: it doesn't print any. Do not, therefore, expect the press associations or the press to be what they are not. Recognize the limitations that they must impose on themselves.

☆ 4 ☆

SYNDICATES AND COLUMNISTS

☆ ☆ ☆ ☆ ☆

NEWSPAPERS can no more get along without syndicates than they can get along without press associations. The press association provides a service which no single newspaper could afford to maintain on its own. The syndicate provides high-priced writers and features on the same basis. Sometimes syndicated writers cover the same ground as the press associations; sometimes, too, they cover the same ground as the staff writers for individual papers. But the main thing the special writer or the special feature has to offer is a point of view, a name, a service that cannot be exactly duplicated anywhere else. Indeed, many newspapers give as much space to syndicated features as they do to press-association news.

Press-association dispatches usually play up the name of the association and omit or play down the name of the author. Syndicate features, on the other hand, play up the name of the author and play down the name of the syndicate. For a syndicate is primarily a sales organization that places all kinds of features in newspapers throughout the country. It is not a news-gathering agency; indeed, most of the material it sells is not news at all. Thus, a syndicate does not have to meet the enormous overhead costs of a news-gathering organization. Its principal job is to line up and build up special writers, cartoonists, celebrities, and specialists and then sell their work as widely as possible. A syndicate lays no great emphasis on editorial policy. Indeed, the same syndicate will often sell features that express diametrically opposite points of view.

Hearst's King Features is the largest syndicate in the country. It specializes, as most syndicates do, in various forms of entertainment that have little bearing on the news or its interpretation. International News Service, it is true, is a subsidiary of King Features, and to that extent, therefore, King Features does have a hand in distributing news. But since both King Features and INS belong to the Hearst empire, their policy is not governed by their relationship to each other but by their relationship to Hearst. It is somewhat the same story with the Scripps-Howard organization which controls the United Press and which also has two syndicates—the Newspaper Enterprise Association and United Features. The difference is that the United Press does a slightly more objective reporting job than INS; but its two syndicates handle the work of writers who come nearer to expressing Scripps-Howard policy than the INS writers do to expressing Hearst policy. Finally, the Associated Press, most powerful of the news-gathering agencies, pays least attention to the syndication of special articles and feature writers. It has, however, an

Associated Press Feature Service, but this is a membership proposition like all the rest of the Associated Press service.

Individual newspapers syndicate individual writers. The *New York Herald Tribune* sells the Dorothy Thompson and Walter Lippmann columns throughout the United States. The North American Newspaper Alliance, set up on a co-operative basis and specializing in *New York Times* contributors and the writings of eminent foreigners, is not, however, a *Times* subsidiary. It operates on the same general lines as the Associated Press.

What concerns you as a newspaper reader is not the syndicate that an article or a feature comes from but the person who writes it. By and large, no writer of power or influence acts as the conscious mouthpiece for any interest. An alert syndicate will naturally urge its writers to write the kind of stuff that will sell. Newspapers also prefer to hire writers who attract readers. The writers, in turn, bear in mind what their public likes and what sort of thing their employers want them to say. The words you read in the paper thus embody a triple compromise between what the newspaper proprietor wants, what the public is supposed to want, and what the writer actually believes. The most influential writers, however, write from conviction, not at dictation; so when you see something especially effective in print, do not assume that it is a put-up job.

Dorothy Thompson, the most talked-about columnist of recent years, illustrates perfectly what I have in mind. Her opinions and recommendations change like a pinwheel. One day she writes an open letter to Congress demanding an immediate declaration of war on Germany at a time when she knows that more than 90 per cent of the American people oppose such a move. Then, a few weeks later, she describes as "insane" anyone who suggests our sending troops abroad: it seems we are not nearly ready to fight this war she wanted to declare a few weeks before. And the next thing you know she will be attacking the irresponsibility of the people she disagrees with that day.

Whatever you may think of this performance, it is utterly sincere and independent. A psychologist might be able to offer an interesting interpretation of Miss Thompson's political behavior; Freud will perhaps go a lot farther than Marx in accounting for it. Ancestry may also play some small part. Although she proclaims herself an American of the Americans, Miss Thompson is the daughter of English parents. Her father was an English clergyman who met her mother, who was also English, while on a brief visit to the United States. Their marriage, however, decided them both to settle here, and it was therefore in an English household, transplanted to American soil, that Miss Thompson grew up. Since graduating from Vassar, she has spent more time abroad than she has in the United States. Her first husband was Hungarian. Her accent, a hodgepodge of Middle Westernisms and Anglicisms—she almost always remembers to say "Ameddican"—reflects a personality, split as so many American personalities are, between the New World and the Old.

But the chief difference between Dorothy Thompson and other American journalists who have spent most of their lives abroad is one of degree, not of kind. Most Americans derive most of their culture from Europe; many Americans have personal ties with the Old World as well. Thus, if you take any American and set him up as a newspaper correspondent in any European capital, he will quickly become susceptible to that capital. Whether it is Paris, London, or Vienna, he will make friends there. He will become an expert on that neck of the woods. Not only will he become a sentimental partisan of the country in which he is working; he will acquire a vested interest in that country. He will want to see it and his friends there prosper.

An American, brought up, as many of us are, on European values, succumbs easily to this atmosphere. A few, however, resist, but the odds are against them. It isn't a question of a conflict between American and European culture; Americans accept so many European values anyway that there isn't any conflict at all. No American correspondent of any consequence has fallen for Hitler; the Nazi revolution seems to be foreign to the American temperament. Indeed, American journalists stationed in Berlin have got into more trouble than the journalists of any other country. Dorothy Thompson was refused admission to the Third Reich, yet she has said with perfect truth, "I am one of the few real pro-Germans in this country."

When Sir Nevile Henderson became British ambassador to Berlin, he expressed amazement because people accused him of being "pro-German." It never occurred to him, he said, that he was being anything but pro-British. And though Sir Nevile has lived to regret the policies he pursued, he saw no conflict of loyalties and no contradiction when his government stopped appeasing Hitler and declared war. This kind of patriotism is something that few Americans understand. Indeed, we do not call into question the patriotism of our journalists when they announce they are "pro-German," "pro-British," or "pro-French." We assume that they support foreign countries at least as warmly as they support their own. A patriotic Englishman, on the other hand, finds such labels meaningless. Bright or stupid, he remains an Englishman.

Thus, in sizing up any American who writes on foreign affairs, the first question to ask is whether that writer is the partisan of some foreign country or some foreign political movement. Dorothy Thompson is pro-German and anti-Nazi. No refugee from the Third Reich hopes and works more passionately for the downfall of Hitler. Miss Thompson's ancestry also predisposes her in favor of Britain. She takes counsel from Dr. Gustav Stolper, former editor of the leading economic weekly in Germany, from Harold Nicolson, now British Minister of Information, and from such local Anglophiles as Hamilton Fish Armstrong and Raymond Gram Swing. But Miss Thompson's voice is not the voice of the British Foreign Office, speaking in a slightly garbled American accent. It is the voice of a Europeanized American, British colonial by ancestry and German refugee by choice.

Walter Lippmann is quite a different story. He is no returned expatriate but the eternal intellectual in search of a faith. In 1910, he emerged from Harvard a mild Socialist, but he soon supported Woodrow Wilson and the League of Nations. Throughout the 1920's he remained a consistent Democrat, voting for Cox in 1920, for Davis in 1924, for Smith in 1928, and continually preaching internationalism in the leading editorials that he wrote for the New York World. By the 1930's, when The World came to an end and the depression steadily deepened, Lippmann found comfort in the society of Thomas W. Lamont and discovered a great statesman in the person of the late Dwight W. Morrow. It was at this point that the Ogden Reids who control the New York Herald Tribune felt they could safely open the columns of that paper to Walter Lippmann's liberalism three days a week. The depression had President Hoover and the editorial writers on the Herald Tribune baffled and it seemed that Lippmann might have some new angles on the situation.

And for a while Walter Lippmann did his duty. On the eve of the 1932 Democratic convention he declared that Franklin Roosevelt was just a pleasant chap who happened to want very much to be President; he preferred the sterner stuff of which Newton D. Baker was made, and during the convention a Lippmann column endorsing the Baker candidacy was distributed to every delegate. But Lipp-

48

mann's endorsement of Baker had the same magical effect as his endorsements of Davis, Cox, and Smith in successive presidential contests. Mr. Baker fell by the wayside, and in 1936 the unerring Lippmann instinct found in Alf Landon the ideal presidential candidate.

Testy critics of Lippmann's career have accused him of opportunism. Corliss Lamont once identified him as the midget who sat on J. P. Morgan's knee. These strictures are worse than unfair; they are inaccurate. Far from excelling as a picker of winners, Lippmann appears to be almost a connoisseur of lost causes—from Socialism in 1910 to Alf Landon in 1936. Moreover, when he has to choose between personal advantage and loyalty to the lost cause, it is the lost cause that wins every time. After all, the Ogden Reids did not hire him to write Republican editorials for them; their own staff takes care of that. Mr. Lippmann was hired as a kind of professional heretic—at any rate by *Herald Tribune* standards. But no sooner was he safely established than he dropped his Democratic heresy and became an orthodox Republican.

Because Walter Lippmann and other successful newspapermen associate with the rich and powerful, it is sometimes assumed that they do not speak their own minds. But this is not the way things work at all. Lippmann expresses a point of view that has often coincided with the Morgan point of view. Often but not always: Walter Lippmann criticized the Morgan preferred lists in 1933. In other words, when you read a Lippmann column, you are not reading a disguised publicity release from 23 Wall Street. You are not even reading what Walter Lippmann thinks the Anglophile plutocrats of the Eastern seaboard would say if they had his gift of expression. Too often he hits the nail on J. P. Morgan's thumb; the editorial page of *The New York Times* speaks with much more authority. But Walter Lippmann is a lot easier to read—partly because he has a great gift for writing, partly because he is honestly trying to write the truth as he sees it. If he sees the world through "Made in England" glasses, is that his fault?

Dorothy Thompson and Walter Lippmann have more influence and more readers than any other political columnists. They do not, however, have as wide a following as two other columnists who only occasionally write about politics—Walter Winchell and Westbrook Pegler. Winchell is the bright, particular star in the Hearst firmament, and in addition to writing a daily gossip column he talks once a week over the radio. Winchell never steps squarely on Mr. Hearst's toes, but he has his own political views. These views are perhaps largely determined by the fact that Walter Winchell was a New York boy who went into vaudeville in his teens along with Eddie Cantor and George Jessel. He is the tin-pan alley patriot of 1940— sentimental, flag-waving, alternately intolerant and warm-hearted, a streamlined version of George M. Cohan's "Yankee Doodle Dandy." At one time, Winchell suspected Dorothy Thompson of concealed Fascist tendencies; now he is her male counterpart among the Hitler haters.

Walter Winchell is as much the product of one environment as Walter Lippmann is the product of another. One has been conditioned by Broadway, the other by Park Avenue; both express their conditioning—honestly, spontaneously, brilliantly. Both also exemplify the prevailing morals and customs of the circles in which they move. Walter Winchell is passionately devoted to his two children; he is obsessed with the fear of kidnapers and has his family closely guarded. He also takes a bodyguard with him on many of his rounds. Yet in spite of his affection for his family, Winchell's connections with the underworld and the large proportion of false rumors that he has put into circulation suggest that his virtues have their limits. During the summer of 1940 *The New Yorker* printed a series of articles by St. Clair McKelway, revealing some of the less savory details of Winchell's career. A few feeble rejoinders in Winchell's column, entitled "Now It's My Turn," did not meet the carefully documented case history that McKelway assembled.

But the archdefender of virtue is Westbrook Pegler, self-appointed spokesman of the "kids-having" type of American. Born and educated in the Catholic faith, Pegler has frequently criticized the many divorces among President Roosevelt's children, and now that he is earning about $60,000 a year he opposes high taxes as much as if he were a millionaire. Pegler, however, was born into the newspaper business. Son of an Irish-Canadian mother and of an English newspaperman who has spent most of his life in the United States, Pegler never was graduated from high school, but went to work at the age of sixteen as an office boy in the Chicago bureau of the United Press. He has remained in newspaper work ever since, making his early reputation as a sports writer, then as a sports columnist, and finally as a general columnist.

Pegler's columns reflect Scripps-Howard policy much more clearly than Winchell's columns reflect Hearst policy. This is not to say that Pegler ever writes against his convictions. As a self-made man who came to the top the hard way, he needs no prompting to share many of the views of his employer, Roy Howard, on the subject of taxation, labor unions, and relief. Yet behind Pegler's elaborately hard-boiled manner there is a certain uneasiness, a kind of inferiority complex even. In a long article on Pegler in the September 14, 1940, *Saturday Evening Post*, Jack Alexander observed, "He seems to have perceived early that, in the nature of things, there was an implied warfare between himself and the world. This defensive spirit of hands-off-Pegler-if-you-don't-want-to-get-socked survives to this day."

Jack Alexander also commented on the Pegler-Winchell feud, and, sure enough, as soon as his article appeared Winchell reported with delight that Alexander had found Pegler abnormally thin-skinned. And Pegler has often ribbed Winchell about his irresponsible gossip, his emotionalism, his arrival in journalism by way of show business. Yet these spats between widely read columnists show how the people who influence public opinion are themselves influenced and how their own opinions are formed. Just as Dorothy Thompson and Walter Lippmann reflect their polite backgrounds and associations, so Walter Winchell and Westbrook Pegler speak for a different set of backgrounds and associates. Exactly because neither Winchell nor Pegler received even so much as a high-school education they speak and write the language of the common man. But because they earn at least as much money as their high-brow competitors, they approve as warmly as the high-brows do of a social order in which they have flourished. Indeed, they are perhaps more conservative than the high-brows, more set against change because they have traveled farther to reach the positions they enjoy today.

But the most conservative of all the general columnists writing in the United States came to this country from England. Boake Carter is now a naturalized citizen who far prefers his adopted country to his country of origin. The son of Anglo-Irish parents, he was born in Russia, forty-two years ago, his father having worked in the British Civil Service. Carter does not wear an old-school tie; he attended one of the humbler Cambridge colleges— Christ's; he flew in the Royal Air Force during the last war and came to the United States in 1920. Here he entered the oil business, getting what jobs he could as an engineer in Oklahoma, Texas, Mexico, and Central America.

In 1923 Carter became a reporter for the *Tulsa World* and spent the next nine years working for various newspapers all the way from Mexico City to Philadelphia. Then, in 1932, he became one of the first radio news commentators and soon attracted an enormous following. Originally he criticized Hoover and supported Roosevelt, but as time went on he turned against Roosevelt's foreign policy, and got himself in wrong with labor by criticizing the CIO's organization of the maritime workers. Carter has always opposed meddling in the Orient or in Europe and has written a book on each of these two subjects. But his British ancestry and his experience in the oil industry have made him a thumping American imperialist as far as the New World is concerned.

Boake Carter might be described as the British equivalent of the occasional American who drops his American citizenship—and, if possible, his American accent—becomes a British subject more royalist than the King, and abuses the land of his birth. No native-born American can achieve such heights of patriotic fervor as this naturalized Englishman; no corn-fed yokel hates and suspects the British Empire so bitterly as this ex-Britisher who knows the seamier sides of British imperialism at first hand. Of course, Boake Carter's Irish ancestry may account for some of his anti-British sentiment, just as he probably inherits his conservatism from his civil-servant father. But just as

54

the British occasionally Americanize themselves by marrying Americans or admitting Americans to British citizenship, so the United States has Anglicized itself via Boake Carter who, for all his attacks on the Empire, remains an Englishman and only regrets that more Americans are not so English as himself.

Eleanor Roosevelt, whose column appears every day in the Scripps-Howard papers (and many others), is the complete antithesis of Boake Carter in every respect. To tell her story would take a book. The one thing a reader of her column might bear in mind is that Mrs. Roosevelt sometimes releases trial balloons for her husband, and when she writes about politics she almost always expresses a point of view that has the blessing of the White House. Needless to say her opinions bear no resemblance to the opinions of the Scripps-Howard syndicate that distributes her column.

General Hugh S. Johnson, on the other hand, often lays down the Scripps-Howard line; on some occasions, indeed, he anticipates it. Although he has a soft spot in his heart for Bernard M. Baruch with whom he worked during the last war, the General criticizes the President more vigorously than any other writer of comparable influence—except, perhaps, Boake Carter. From the turn of the century on through the First World War, General Johnson made a successful career for himself in the Army. He graduated from West Point and rose to the rank of Brigadier General. But during the war he devoted himself to desk work, organizing the civilian draft, and after the war he went into business. He has always had a flair for writing, but his point of view remains that of the military man. This does not mean that he has the rigid "brass hat" philosophy or that he is a slave to red tape. It means that he stands for organization and discipline. Whereas an occasional army officer like General Leonard Wood will refresh the military establishment by bringing to it the civilian point of view, General Johnson brings the military point of view into civilian life—and into his newspaper column.

Next to Westbrook Pegler and General Johnson, William Philip Simms and Raymond Clapper are the two most widely read correspondents on the Scripps-Howard payroll. Simms lives in Washington but writes about foreign affairs. Clapper also lives in Washington and specializes on national politics. Simms belongs to the pre-war generation. Born fifty-nine years ago in Georgia, he received his education in his native state and got his first job on the *Atlanta Constitution*. The next year he moved to Cincinnati and by 1908 he had become managing editor of the *Cincinnati Post*. From 1909 to 1914 he represented the United Press in Paris, spent the next two years as a war correspondent, and then covered the Peace Conference for the United Press. Simms left the United Press for a year to head the International News Service bureau at Washington, but he returned to the United Press for a tour of the Far East before he covered the Washington

Naval Conference of 1921–22. Since that time, he has written on foreign affairs and traveled extensively.

It would be hard to find a better-trained reporter and interpreter of world news, yet in the spring of 1940 Simms made a really spectacular bust reporting the war in France. It was the same bust that almost all the other newspapermen made, but because of his professional eminence Simms bears an especially heavy responsibility. On May 27 Simms cabled a story from London which began as follows: "Five hundred fighter planes just now might turn the tide of battle in Flanders. Five hundred American fighter planes delivered in the course of the next two weeks might conceivably change the course of European history," and later in the same dispatch he wrote, "In a previous dispatch I said that a thousand planes now would be worth two thousand next month or four thousand next fall. I wish to amend that statement. Five hundred planes now would be worth two thousand a month hence."

Note that these pronouncements emanated from London. What was the real position in France at the time? On August 19, 1940, Ludovic Oscar Frossard who held the post of Minister of Information and Propaganda in the Reynaud Cabinet stated that on May 16—eleven days before Simms wrote from London—the French government had already given up France for lost. And on July 3, 1940, Simms confirmed his own error. "France was licked before the war started," he wrote. "She never had a Chinaman's chance. And it wasn't the Nazis that licked her. It

57

was her own politicians, some of them incompetent, some soft, some highly visionary."

Far from reflecting on the ability or integrity of William Philip Simms as a foreign correspondent, this exploit added to his reputation. Edgar Ansel Mowrer had made just the same mistake and was thereupon judged competent by his employer, Colonel Frank Knox, to collaborate with William J. Donovan on a series of newspaper articles about Fifth Column activities in Europe. Vincent Sheean presents a somewhat similar spectacle. After the Soviet invasion of Poland he wrote two articles for *The New Republic* and declared at the end of the first, "In my own case, these two articles will constitute the first criticism I have ever made of the Soviet Union and the first time I have been willing to discuss Stalin (or even, in fact, to mention him) in print." Yet throughout the 1930's Sheean had written for newspapers of every political complexion and was held in especially high esteem among the liberals although he systematically refused to criticize or even mention the name of one of the foremost statesmen of that period. And this confession of self-censorship did no more damage to his career than Simms had been damaged by his performance in France.

The whole point here is not that Simms, Mowrer, or Sheean is guilty of moral turpitude or even of incompetence. Indeed, their reputations for integrity and ability never stood higher than after they had committed and acknowledged these egregious professional blunders. The point I am driving at is that the modern journalist operates under a code that is all his own. A scientist who admits that he ignores important data or a scientist who confesses that he has drawn conclusions on the basis of false evidence is not, customarily, awarded high honors for his shortcomings. But a journalist who makes an honest mistake or a journalist who deliberately censors himself because of his devotion to some nonjournalistic value suffers no setback. On the contrary. He talks over the radio, writes for the big-money magazines, and delivers lectures at higher prices than ever before.

What it all comes down to is not that modern journalism sets a premium on inaccuracy. What it comes down to is that accuracy has become a matter of secondary concern. Newspaper readers want excitement; they want personalities; they do not blame a correspondent if he makes an honest mistake or if his idealism occasionally wafts him off into the Cloud-Cuckoo-Land of wishful thinking. Dullness is the only unforgivable sin.

☆ 5 ☆

WASHINGTON NEWS

☆ ☆ ☆ ☆ ☆

THE CAPITAL of the world's mightiest nation is always the
capital of the world's news. For over a century, London
occupied that position. Today, Washington has taken its
place. To understand world news you must therefore
understand Washington news, and to understand Washington news it helps a lot if you have some idea of how
that news is gathered.

No less than five hundred journalists are admitted to the
press galleries of Congress: they represent nearly three
hundred different newspapers and news agencies. *The
New York Times* alone has nineteen regular correspondents in the national capital as compared with only seven
in 1925. These correspondents have many different jobs
to do. Some of them attend the sessions of Congress;
others have regular assignments to pick up news at the
different government departments; others attend the innumerable hearings and investigations that are forever in
progress. But these are routine affairs and the government
does its best to make information available to the press
through written statements, interviews, and regular news

releases. A correspondent's real skill comes in when he must interpret this news and uncover fresh sources. It is therefore the business of every Washington correspondent to cultivate important people who can give him personal information and opinion and it is also the business of the Washington correspondent to know when to use and when not to use the material he picks up.

A booklet, entitled "Covering Washington," issued by *The New York Times* defines the correspondent's problem this way: "The correspondent's task is to get all the news, and get it accurately. But a sixth sense of journalism must tell him what to print and what not, when to 'shoot the works' and when to hold his fire. He must keep faith and respect confidences. He must know without being told when a politician's words are not for publication and, on the other hand, when a politician wants news to get out without being directly quoted as the source. He must know where to look for gold, and how to recognize it when he sees it."

The same booklet gives the case history of how the *Times* scored a scoop by applying these principles. A government official who had given a *Times* man several tips told him one morning in confidence that the United States was preparing to denounce its treaty of trade and friendship with Japan later that same day. This enabled the *Times* to get the whole background of the story written and set up in type so that when the news was officially released at ten o'clock that night, the *Times* had it completely covered in its earliest edition. If the correspondent had violated the confidence and let the story out prematurely, he could never have hoped for another favor from the same official—or, indeed, from anyone else. And, by the same token, the official who gave the *Times* the correct information in advance knew he could count on the closest kind of co-operation and the friendliest kind of interpretation. Incidents of this kind are occurring every day and explain the strict and special code of ethics that governs all relations between the press and the government.

It is a relationship furthermore that works two ways. President Hoover suffered agonies, and his administration received cruel handling in the press, because he refused to hold informal press conferences with the Washington correspondents, discussing some points "off the record" and answering other questions point-blank for publication. Roosevelt, on the other hand, owes an immeasurable amount of his popularity to the newspapers. From the very start he has taken newspapermen into his confidence, made their work easier for them, and been repaid in any number of friendly stories. Actually, of course, the press conference is not as informal as it looks in the photographs. For years President Roosevelt dodged every kind of question on the third term. As far as that issue was concerned there might just as well not have been any press conferences at all. And Roosevelt's refusal to face up to that issue worked against his best interests—though on a relatively small scale—just as Hoover's refusal to answer any face-to-face questions hurt him irreparably with the press and the country at large. After all, the official who holds a press conference can exercise a great deal of control over what is discussed and complete control over what is printed. Therefore, the official who holds no press conferences or who systematically refuses to discuss certain subjects leaves the door wide open for his hostile critics to circulate any rumors they please. A straight answer to even the most embarrassing question usually does much less harm in the long run.

The first point to bear in mind about Washington news is that the officials want the news to reach the public and have arranged a great many facilities to make that news available. The second point to bear in mind about Washington news is that it is gathered and interpreted by human beings whose writings reflect their personalities, loyalties, and interests. These two considerations apply to all Washington correspondents, but here I am concerned only with those who write syndicated news or a syndicated column for a nation-wide audience, and I shall not even try to cover all of them. I am simply selecting some of the more influential and representative newspaper people in the national capital.

No member of the Washington press corps rates higher among his colleagues than Raymond Clapper. This stoop-shouldered, forty-eight-year-old Kansan got his start on the *Kansas City Star* in 1916 and had long experience on other Midwestern newspapers before coming to Washington as chief Scripps-Howard correspondent and columnist in the national capital. Mr. Clapper endorsed most of the New Deal until the Supreme Court plan and the third-term issue came up. Always a Republican at heart, he is a "right of center" liberal who distrusted Roosevelt's foreign policy until the Germans invaded the Low Countries. Since then he has gone, with diminishing reluctance, along with the Washington war party, although he advocates a kind of limited imperialism rather than direct intervention in Europe.

But there is one respect in which Mr. Clapper differs from his colleagues in the national capital. He does not believe that God has summoned him personally to save the American people. I have already referred to the tendency of American correspondents abroad to indentify themselves with the country in which they are stationed. Washington has the same kind of effect—but with this difference. Whereas the American correspondent abroad must always remain on the outside looking in, the Washington correspondent can enjoy the illusion that he is directly shaping national policy. Any widely read writer who works close to people wielding great political power soon develops an itch to exercise some of that power himself. The foreign correspondent must operate indirectly by influencing American opinion. The Washington correspondent, on the other hand, can operate directly. The Washington correspondent can do more than relay to the public the views of his favorite statesman. He can actually formulate those views himself.

This is the way it works. Many of our Senators, for example, lack the time to issue statements on all the great issues of the day; some of them lack the ability; none of them, however, lack hangers-on among the newspapermen. These hangers-on are always delighted to express the views of our great statesmen for them or, if the statesmen have no views, to supply not only the phrasing but the ideas as well. Washington correspondents thus find themselves turning out radio broadcasts, addresses delivered before Congress, and all sorts of official and unofficial statements that seem to come from our political leaders. Washington correspondents also use their typewriters to send up trial balloons. Sometimes the correspondent supplies the idea; sometimes it originates with the political leader. Usually—though not always—the trial balloon is preceded by the statement, "authoritative sources declare," or, "it was learned today from a source that has hitherto proved unimpeachable." The quotation or interpretation that follows can always be regarded as the view of some important personage who does not want to go on record at that particular moment.

This procedure occurs more often in news dispatches than in syndicated columns. Washington columnists acquire such self-importance that they regard their own writings as having almost the character of state papers. This applies especially to those columnists who express the point of view of the administration in power. And when a proadministration columnist does not actually express the view of some important government official, he is apt to express a view that he hopes the government will adopt.

Syndicated Washington columns, especially the proadministration ones, therefore deserve reading. Only when an administration is clearly on the skids, as was the case during the last two years of Hoover, does the antiadministration columnist speak for anything except an opposition that wants the jobs the other fellows have. Thus, under the New Deal, we find that the pro-Roosevelt columns have the greatest influence and readership. These include Jay Franklin, Ernest K. Lindley, Pearson and Allen, Alsop and Kintner. The opposition columnists include Hearst's Paul Mallon, Mark Sullivan of the *New York Herald Tribune*, Arthur Krock of *The New York Times*, David Lawrence, and Frank Kent.

But conscription, the defense program, the drift toward war, and the widespread demand for "national unity" are obliterating many party differences. Republican columnists who support national defense speak with an authority and confidence they have lacked in eight long years. Contrariwise, when Ernest K. Lindley began to wander off the Roosevelt reservation and advocated strict neutrality shortly after the outbreak of the European war, his friend, the President, publicly questioned the veracity of one of his stories. But Mrs. Lindley is a good friend of Mrs. Roosevelt; she holds a job under the New Deal, and today all is forgiven and forgotten.

Even when the British Parliament voted almost dictatorial powers to the Churchill government, the London press did not go totalitarian. Americans are perhaps less tolerant, especially in times of stress, than the British, but in spite of the strong trend toward national unity, the Washington press corps is not likely to turn into a regiment of Charlie McCarthys in any future that we can foresee. The newspaper publishers, the press associations, and the syndicates all have a huge stake in a relatively free press. More uniformity may well become the order of the day; discussion of some topics may be forbidden; but no power on earth is going to stop the Washington columnists from trying to make the country safe for something or other.

As of 1940 and subject to possible change in the next year or two, "Capital Parade" by Joseph Alsop and Robert Kintner is the best-written and most authoritative column coming out of Washington. These two young men—both of them refugees from the Washington bureau of the New York Herald Tribune—now have the inside track to Roosevelt, Welles, Berle, and the so-called "policy-makers" at the State Department. Although less ardent New Dealers than their chief competitors—Jay Franklin, Ernest K. Lindley, and the Pearson-Allen team—Alsop and Kintner scooped the entire working press of Washington with their American White Paper. This pamphlet, publicly praised by the President, came nearer to being an official statement of American foreign policy than anything that saw print between the start of the Second World War and the German invasion of the Low Countries.

How did Alsop and Kintner steal a march on some of the most consistent Roosevelt boosters in the national capital? A Boston lawyer of my acquaintance who sent his two sons to Groton School once remarked that he could never feel real enthusiasm for President Roosevelt because the President had attended Groton—"and no stream can rise higher than its source." Joseph Alsop not only attended both Harvard and Groton; he is himself a Roosevelt, though a closer relation of Eleanor's than of Franklin's. His collaborator, Robert Kintner, was graduated from Swarthmore and once covered Wall Street for the *New York Herald Tribune*.

Thus, what the Alsop-Kintner column expresses is not the messianic wing of the New Deal, with which President Roosevelt has been chiefly identified. Rather do they speak for the conservative Eastern aristocracy into which Roosevelt was born and to which he reverted the moment a serious crisis began to develop abroad. Because Walter Lippmann is neither a Roosevelt nor an Episcopalian, he has never quite achieved the authentic Harvard manner; indeed, it is something that cannot be achieved. You must be born to it as Joseph Alsop and the President were. And it is more than a manner. It is an attitude that the fashionable church schools of the Eastern seaboard inculcate and that Harvard and the better undergraduate clubs

68

fortify. Often, this training unfits its victims for American life. Occasionally, however, a product of Groton and Harvard refuses to conform. He embarks on a career of his own; he competes with the crowd; and once or twice in a generation, one such rebel possesses a mixture of ability, arrogance, and charm that brings him to the top of the heap.

If Jay Franklin had attended Groton instead of St. Mark's, Harvard instead of Yale, and if he had taken the precaution to be related to the Roosevelts instead of being the son of a New England clergyman, he might have written *American White Paper*. As John Franklin Carter, Jr., he once worked for the State Department, where he ruffled the sensitive Mr. Hoover and then returned to his first career as a journalist. As John Carter he wrote a bloodthirsty book entitled *Man Is War*; in 1932 he flirted for a while with Howard Scott's Technocrats. He visited Germany, tried to launch a New National Party of his own, expressed some sympathy for Hitler, not much for Britain. But with the advent of the New Deal he went to work under Tugwell in the Resettlement Administration, discovered Pare Lorentz, and then blossomed out as a daily columnist. Here his gifts as a phrase-maker, his phenomenal energy, and his all-round ability kept him going. "Jay Franklin" speaks for the left wing of the New Deal. Despite his early years in the State Department he writes more about domestic matters than he does about foreign affairs. He is closer to Mrs. Roosevelt than to the President, closer to Harry Hopkins than to Frank Knox. Nothing he has written is quite as official as *American White Paper,* but it all bears the New Deal stamp.

John Franklin Carter, Jr., has always written too much and under too many different names. Even the syndicated column on which most of his reputation now rests carries one of his many pseudonyms. As "Diplomat," he has written detective stories. As "The Unofficial Observer," he has written books on foreign and domestic affairs. As John Carter, he wrote for the Sunday Book Section of *The New York Times.* As Jefferson Chase, he wrote for *Vanity Fair.* It is significant that the most sensitive, personal, and satisfying book he has ever written, *The Rectory Family,* describing his boyhood in Williamstown, Massachusetts, is signed John Franklin Carter, Jr. It is no derogation to his work as a newspaperman to say that this book leaves the impression that literature lost more than journalism gained when John Franklin Carter, Jr., became Jay Franklin.

For sheer journalistic competence, Drew Pearson and Robert Allen show all the other New Deal columnists the way in their "Washington Merry-Go-Round." For one thing, they have had more newspaper experience than any of their rivals; for another their talents complement each other. Allen is an emotional, hard-boiled little man who enlisted in the army in 1916 at the age of sixteen, and he is now so angry with Hitler that he has his wife drilling with a gun. Allen is the leg man of the team; he loves to get a good story even if it lands him in hot water. His collaborator, Drew Pearson, is the perfect foil. Pearson writes well; he prefers to stay at home and gather information by telephone. When he does go out, he frequents embassy parties and salons of an evening. Thanks to their division of labor and their close personal relations with the inner circle of left-wing New Dealers, Pearson and Allen's "Washington Merry-Go-Round" has turned up more exclusive stories than any other column in the national capital.

Mark Sullivan's column is exclusive in a different sense. This sixty-six-year-old dean of the anti-New Dealers is the outstanding professional Republican of the old school. One of the few active newspapermen who was already playing an important role in the Taft-Roosevelt period, Mr. Sullivan owes much of his professional reputation to his prediction of Harding's nomination, long before the 1920 Republican Convention; in fact, he had picked Harding before Harding himself thought he had a look-in. But it was not until 1929 that Mark Sullivan really came into his own, thanks to his close personal friendship with Herbert Hoover. As a loyal Harvard Episcopalian and a former overseer of the university, Sullivan has maintained friendly personal relations with President Roosevelt. A couple of years ago he used to debate the New Deal over the radio with Jay Franklin. Today his column stands like a ruined monument to an age that has gone.

The new generation of anti-New Dealers has no more vigorous spokesman than Paul Mallon, Hearst's key man in Washington. When Mallon worked for the United Press he was known as the greatest living pencil reporter on a running story: he was supposed to be able to take notes with one hand and write the story with the other. But, like many other top-flight reporters, Mallon abandoned straight reporting for the more lucrative job of column writing, and his column now appears in more than 400 newspapers. Although the New Deal Administration has remained in office for almost eight years, there are still plenty of Roosevelt haters in responsible quarters, and Mallon knows how to use the ammunition they give him.

Paul Mallon was born and bred a Catholic. David Lawrence is just as much opposed to the New Deal, but he has abandoned the Jewish faith of his ancestors for Buchmanism and Moral Rearmament. Unlike Mallon, David Lawrence supports Roosevelt's foreign policy. During the first two years of Wilson's first administration Lawrence covered the White House for the Associated Press, and from 1926 to 1933 he headed the *United States Daily* which was entirely devoted to Washington news. He still edits its successor, the *United States News*, a weekly publication, and writes a syndicated daily column of Washington news as well. No reporter in the national capital has a more detailed knowledge of how government functions and who does what and why.

Two of the most effective anti-New Dealers in Washington used to be liberals—Frank Kent of the *Baltimore Sun* and Arthur Krock of *The New York Times*. Kent is a hard-bitten newspaperman, now past sixty, who went to work for the *Sun* in 1898 and has never worked for any other paper since. He and Mencken have always admired each other, but Kent preceded Mencken as a convert to orthodoxy when he became a friend of the Hoovers. He still calls himself a Democrat, but has never had much use for Roosevelt—in this respect, anticipating by a few years his own paper's opposition to the New Deal. Frank Kent has written several books on politics and has preserved a more detached attitude than most Washington correspondents. He also stands out as one of the few Washington correspondents who has never cherished any political ambitions for himself. He has always been content to remain a good newspaperman.

Arthur Krock, head of the Washington bureau of *The New York Times*, is one of the half-dozen people who determine *Times* policy. Four times a week he occupies the fifth column on the *Times* editorial page with his signed department, "In the Nation." This is not a column in the usual sense. It is not syndicated and it expresses the *Times* point of view. Its author got his start in his native city of Louisville back in 1906, and three years later he was representing the *Louisville Times* in Washington. Later he became editorial manager of both the *Times* and the *Courier Journal*, working under the Colonel Henry Watterson regime.

73

With this background Krock came to New York in 1923 as assistant to the president of *The World*. Naturally he was a Democrat, and a Democrat he remained when he moved over to the editorial staff of *The New York Times*. After Roosevelt entered the White House he gave Arthur Krock the first and last exclusive interview any newspaperman ever received under the New Deal, but by 1936 Krock was turning against the administration. He had several altercations with New Deal officials about quotations and interpretations that appeared in his column and rarely did his critics get the last word. Krock loves to dine out, to hobnob with the mighty, to play the role of kingmaker. He helped to build up Joseph Kennedy, but his chief distinction is the key post he holds on the most influential newspaper in America.

But the war in Europe and the national-defense program have transformed Washington as they have transformed everything else. They have all but liquidated the New Deal, and, in consequence, party lines and factional differences are disappearing. No longer are the Washington correspondents divided into two groups—the New Dealers and the anti-New Dealers. National unity has become the slogan of the hour and will remain the slogan of many hours to come.

Only one outstanding Washington correspondent refused to fall in line. Ludwell Denny had spent sixteen years working for various Scripps-Howard enterprises, and shortly before the war broke out he achieved his lifelong

ambition and came to Washington to write a daily syndicated column from the capital. Mr. Denny is an able newspaperman. He had just put the *Indianapolis News* on its
feet and a dozen years before had written two disturbing
books—*We Fight for Oil* and *America Conquers Britain*.
He had what his friends would call a "realistic" grasp of
international affairs; his enemies would call it "cynical."
Anyway, he launched a Washington column, discussing
domestic and foreign issues, writing pretty much as he
pleased. Then came the Battle of France. Anyone in
Washington who hinted that the French might lose or
capitulate—even as late as June 10, the day the President
delivered his Charlottesville "stab in the back" speech—
was branded a Fifth Columnist. This is not just my opinion; the statement appeared in the pro-Roosevelt column
John O'Donnell and Doris Fleeson write for the New York
Daily News. Nevertheless, in this atmosphere, Mr. Denny
went to work on the administration, criticizing its outstanding figures from the President down, singling out Secretary Ickes and Mrs. Roosevelt for special attention. And,
above all, he hammered—as he had been hammering for
months past—on the President's drive toward war.

One column in this vein appeared in the early editions
of the Scripps-Howard papers. Friends congratulated Mr.
Denny; he told them they had not seen anything yet,
asked them to wait until tomorrow. Tomorrow arrived,
but Mr. Denny's column did not. Days passed. His column

did not appear. Finally, after several weeks the Scripps-Howard papers began running a series of articles by Mr. Denny on the defense of the Caribbean and Alaska. And here endeth the first lesson.

☆ EXHIBIT A ☆

THE COLUMNISTS

☆ ☆ ☆ ☆ ☆

To DOCUMENT some of the points I have been making in connection with the columnists in Washington and elsewhere, let me now resort to the same device I used in the opening chapter. There I showed how the three chief news associations and three outstanding columnists would report and interpret the daily sun, moon, and tide schedules issued by the United States Coast and Geodetic Survey. Here let me show how some of the writers who have just been passing in review would handle the same story. And since it is a kind of parade, it would seem appropriate for General Hugh S. Johnson to lead it:

New Deal Janissaries are telling the world they have improved on Joshua who made the sun stand still. They have put one third of the nation on WPA and they think their crackpot Quoddy project will make the tides work for them while the shovel brigade rests its haunches on its padded shovel handles. Now I happen to know more about this subject of sun, moon, and tides than I do about anything else. And I don't need to guess how Donald

77

Duck Ickes is going to take that crack, but it doesn't make a damn bit of difference to me. He can boil me in one of the government's hot-oil cases for all I care.

But what I was getting around to is an afternoon I spent over at the headquarters of the United States Coast and Geodetic Survey. What they told me about the tide currents along the shores of this American continent convinced me that some of these government departments know their stuff in spite of Harry the Morgue. Why, these babies have got the tides and the hours of sunrise and sunset figured out months ahead. I wrote down some of the figures to check up on them but I lost the piece of paper somewhere. I guess the ants in my pants must have chewed it up.

Now if an outfit that calls itself the United States Coast and Geodetic Survey can do this kind of job, what in the hell is the matter with the United States Army? Why in the hell haven't we got conscription? Our Commander in Chief has been talking to Hitler like a cavalry colonel bawling out a shavetail, but you can't fight gangsters with fireside chats, no matter how hot you make them. The fact is that everyone in Washington is out of step with everyone else—except me. Those potbellied Senators cannot hear the army bugle playing reveille; the only tune they know is the mess call and that is music to their ears. But if they don't get their snouts out of the feed trough, they will prove Hitler is right when he says a horned toad

78

can defend itself better than the democracies. Pardon me while I step out and take a load off my stomach.

Pro-New Dealers would of course give the information a different twist. Pearson and Allen's "Washington Merry-Go-Round," for example, would be likely to work out something like this:

Insiders foresee the Willkie-McNary forces blundering badly in their attack on New Deal regimentation. FD's hatchet man, Tommy Corcoran, has been compiling information on all the necessary services rendered by government departments—notably the little-publicized United States Coast and Geodetic Survey. Yet this service, a subsidiary of Morgenthau's Treasury, gives vital information on tides, hours of sunrise and sunset, phases of the moon. If Willkie forces the pace on government interference, FD will counter with a blast in behalf of the Geodetic Survey and should be able to capture the hook-line-and-sinker vote without a landing net. All that will be necessary will be for the FDR voice to intone the hours of the tides and the time of sunrise and sunset and he will have the entire seaboard vote—including the Gulf of Mexico.

The more militant Jay Franklin would be likely to take the offensive on this issue:

Big Wendell (I'll fight the champ) Willkie has talked himself into a hole in the ground from which it will require all the efforts of the Wall Street wrecking crew to extricate him. The big utility executive with the Indiana accent and the Fifth Avenue address said he called up the New York office of the United States Coast and Geodetic Survey to find out what time the tide would be high over the week end as he was planning another cruise on publisher Roy Howard's launch which Mr. Howard insists must be called a yacht in all his newspapers. Willkie complained that the line did not answer although he called it repeatedly and went on to draw attention to the plight of fishermen who could not get this vital information. Calls made by other people at the same time reveal that the offices were open as usual. Subsequently, New Deal publicity sleuths gathered telephone-company records to show that Willkie was calling the wrong number and that the line that did not answer was the office of Commonwealth and Southern where the office workers are striking for a living wage.

Alsop and Kintner, on the other hand, would create a more aristocratic atmosphere:

Adolf A. Berle, Jr., the Metternich of the New Deal, eased his slender, seersucker-clad figure into a chintz-covered chaise longue. It had been a weary day in the high-ceilinged old rooms of that monstrosity of Victorian architecture which harbors our policy-makers of the State Department and the cable readers had been following Bill Bullitt's reports from Europe where, in Berle's brilliant

80

phrase, "a world has gone mad." As usual the Bullitt cables contained greetings to Sistie and Buzzie Dall and fond inquiries about the health of the Berles' Siamese cat so that it caused no undue perturbation when a kindly reference to that grizzled old patriot, Marshal Pétain, was followed by the announcement that the moon would enter its first quarter on August 10 and would be full on August 17.

Subsequent investigation, however, revealed that the Berles' Japanese butler had posed as a Japanese agent and thus wormed his way into the bowels of a Nazi Trojan horse. This Trojan horse had penetrated the offices of the United States Coast and Geodetic Survey and had succeeded in tapping the State Department's cable line to Europe. For months past, the Nazi spies had been intercepting Ambassador Bullitt's cables and had used the Berles' Japanese butler to compose bogus messages which were relayed instead. The butler finally tipped off the State Department by putting one of the Coast and Geodetic Survey's regular news bulletins on the wire. Arrests quickly followed, but the most remarkable feature of the situation is that State Department officials privately declare that Bill Bullitt's cables never made so much sense as those composed by the Berles' Japanese butler.

Now let us see how this same story would be handled by three outstanding anti-New Dealers. Arthur Krock would be likely to interpret it this way:

No department of government does a better job, year in year out, than the United States Coast and Geodetic Survey. Quietly, unobtrusively, and with a deadly efficiency that stands out in sorry contrast to the high jinks of our more picturesque New Dealers, it makes vital information available to all and sundry. Look at the Shipping News and you will find set forth in orderly fashion the exact time of sunrise and sunset, the hours of high and low water, the phases of the moon. A trained civil service recording the facts of nature should be the model which all government departments—especially the Treasury—should adopt as their own.

Mark Sullivan would be likely to strike a more ominous note:

The pattern of European dictatorship, already clearly outlined in most of our New Deal agencies, repeats itself in disturbing shape in many quarters and has, in fact, flourished for many years. When the Post Office Department extended its operations to include the parcel post, it struck a deadly blow at sturdy private enterprise as embodied in the various express companies. These companies are not headed by political appointees and therefore they yield a profit to their shareholders whereas the iniquitous parcel-post system permits the shiftless and the incompetent to send packages at less than cost while the industrious taxpayer literally pays the freight.

The United States Coast and Geodetic Survey offers

another example of government interference with private enterprise. This department of government releases free of charge to anyone who asks for it valuable information concerning the tides, the hours of sunrise and sunset, and the like. As a matter of principle I prefer not to state what these hours are although I have them at my side in a press-release sheet especially prepared by the government. If I were to give my column over to gratuitous information compiled by a government bureau (probably incompetent) when such work could be handled by an efficient and honorable private corporation, I should feel as if I were operating under the heel of Stalin's dictatorship in Moscow. Thank God for the Republican Party and may He have mercy on Fair Harvard which has given the nation only a Roosevelt to fill the office that Herbert Hoover once adorned.

Paul Mallon's column, "The News Behind the News," would approach the story from still another angle:

A scandal that will shake New Deal Washington to its foundations is now brewing in the United States Coast and Geodetic Survey. If you are a fisherman or a farmer you know the service this department performs in its daily releases, giving the hours of sunrise and sunset and a tide schedule for all the key seaports of the nation. But unless you have swapped stories with the political tradesmen of Washington, especially those close to the Willkie board of strategy, you do not know that this is the first government department exclusively operated by members of the Roosevelt family. One of the most sensational disclosures that Wendell Willkie promises to make before the end of his campaign is that no less than three hundred and forty-eight Hyde Park Roosevelts and one hundred and sixteen Roosevelts of the Oyster Bay variety have found permanent jobs for themselves in this department during the past eight months. Of course, they have secured these jobs under assumed names—a device they learned, naturally enough, from the Communist Party. It will be recalled that a Pittsburgh Communist enrolled in the Communist Party under the name of Franklin D. Roosevelt. In like fashion, hundreds of Roosevelts are now entering permanent government employment under false names.

6

OUR FOREIGN NEWS AND WHERE IT COMES FROM

☆ ☆ ☆ ☆ ☆

In Washington the approach of war has obliterated many differences between individual correspondents. In Europe the arrival of war has obliterated many correspondents entirely. As the war has spread from one country to another and as the fear of war takes tighter hold on the few countries that have remained neutral, one news bureau after another has had to close up shop; one correspondent after another has had to pack up and come home. In September, 1940, The New York Times discontinued its Moscow bureau because it had not been able to get through any real news since January. The United Press and the Associated Press remain on the job, but all they can send is so strictly censored that they have been reduced to the role of telegraph offices through which the Soviet government releases the news it wants the outside world to read.

France has of course dried up almost completely. News from occupied territory must be sent through Berlin. News from unoccupied France is as carefully censored as news from Germany. Many correspondents who have spent years, decades, even their whole lives in Paris, have ceased functioning. London remains the one important news center in Europe. It has an eccentric censorship but an intelligent one. Sweden, although not a belligerent, watches over the news that goes out of the country almost as carefully as belligerent Italy. In consequence, the role of the American correspondent in Europe is shrinking almost to the vanishing point.

Let me repeat two points I have already made about American correspondents in Europe. One is their tendency to regard themselves as ambassadors to the United States from the country in which they are stationed. The other is their almost universal sympathy for democratic countries, their almost universal antipathy toward dictatorships. Many American correspondents have been chased out of Berlin, Rome, and Moscow. Few have been compelled to leave London or Paris. But as the German armies conquered more and more of Europe, the American correspondents found themselves in a singularly awkward position. Many of them had spent the best part of their lives in countries that have either been swallowed up by Germany or that continue to exist only on German sufferance. In other words, since Hitler launched his conquest of Poland, he has gradually destroyed—among other things—the stake that countless American correspondents had been building up for themselves abroad. As long ago as 1933, Hitler began to destroy the stake that American correspondents had been building up in Germany. With the Nazis in power, all the friendships, contacts, and ideas that American correspondents had developed through their association with Hitler's enemies proved worse than useless. Indeed, one reason why this country has so long been so shockingly misinformed about Germany is that most of the correspondents who sent us our news from that country had no contact with the Hitler movement.

As long as the Germans continue to dominate the European continent, Berlin will supersede Paris and London as the center of European news. This means that most American correspondents with European experience are out of a job for the duration of the war—and perhaps for good if Germany wins. In other words, few Americans have a larger personal, material stake in a British victory than the great majority of our foreign correspondents who see, in a Hitler triumph, the loss of their own bread and butter.

I have perhaps oversimplified the situation and stated it too crudely, but even if we take a more idealistic view, we see the same picture. In fact, if we look upon our correspondents as so many knights-errant—and they have no one to blame but themselves if we do see them in that role—it is impossible to imagine any of them ever being able to function under any kind of dictatorship. Whereas the New Deal correspondents in Washington change principles as hastily as the politicians and thus preserve contact with their news sources, our correspondents abroad

87

have not compromised with their principles and have lost their jobs in consequence.

What is the job of a foreign correspondent and how does he do it? We have already seen how the Washington press corps works, and the same general principles used to apply in foreign capitals. At the present time, however, conditions abroad are so different from conditions in Washington that the comparison does not really get us very far. One principle, however, holds equally good in war and peace, in America and Europe. It is the principle of respecting the source from which the news comes. An American correspondent in a foreign capital must have that same sixth sense about handling the important people from whom he gets his news as the American correspondent in Washington. The main difference is that American correspondents abroad have less initiative about building up contacts with important foreign statesmen, and the statesmen, in their turn, naturally do not cultivate American correspondents as eagerly as they cultivate their own. The British, of course, offer an exception to this rule. For one thing, there is no barrier of language; for another, the British do not underestimate the importance of a good press in the United States.

The American correspondent abroad makes the same rounds of the same official news sources as the American correspondent in Washington. Press conferences on the Roosevelt model are almost unheard of abroad; the Europeans go in more heavily for written statements and propaganda handouts which the correspondents too often rehash and send out as news. But there is no American correspondent abroad who does not read the local papers carefully. He quotes these papers in his dispatches and it is his business to know what each paper represents— who owns it, who writes for it, how close it stands to the government. It is also the business of the American correspondent abroad to associate with the people in the country where he is stationed. Social activities play as large a part as they do in Washington, and the conscientious correspondent will also read up on historical background.

And the more conscientiously a correspondent follows this routine, the more "Europeanized" he becomes. At the present time, therefore, he finds himself in a triple predicament. In the first place, he must remember he is writing for American readers and must not lose touch with the American point of view. In the second place, he must saturate himself as thoroughly as possible in a foreign atmosphere. And in the third place, the foreign atmosphere in which he has so thoroughly saturated himself is probably undergoing a dubious air-conditioning treatment at the hands of Hitler who releases fumes that no American, and above all no Anglicized or Gallicized American, can breathe.

It can be seen, then, that many American correspondents work under impossible conditions, and many more fear that they will soon share the fate of their comrades whom Hitler has driven out of one capital after another —Berlin, Vienna, Prague, and Paris. Meanwhile, the correspondents who still function do two jobs. They report the news and they interpret it. Some, of course, lay the emphasis on the reporting. This holds more true of the Associated Press than of the United Press correspondents. The general tendency, however, is to go in more for interpretation. It depends on the individual. It depends on whom he is working for. It depends on the country in which he is working.

The Associated Press, true to its tradition of anonymity and its preference for straight reporting, has only one big conspicuous personality abroad. He is Louis P. Lochner, head of the Berlin bureau, whose name frequently appears on his dispatches. Mr. Lochner comes of Midwest German stock. His father was a clergyman; his mother's maiden name was von Haugwitz. Before the last war he was a professional lecturer on peace; when war broke out he served as Henry Ford's secretary aboard the famous peace ship. He then became secretary to the Conference for Continuous Mediation at Stockholm and The Hague, and after the war he spent a year editing the International Labor News Service. It was with this background that Mr. Lochner went to work for the Associated Press in 1919. His first wife died in 1920 and two years later he married a German.

In 1928, Mr. Lochner became head of the Berlin Bureau of the Associated Press and he has held the job ever since.

Because of his marriage and because the Nazis have let him stay on the job after they had kicked out Dorothy Thompson, Edgar Mowrer, Otto Tolischus, and many other newspaper luminaries, Mr. Lochner has been accused of playing the Nazi game. But he faced a choice of evils. Either he could toe the line and hold his job or he could overstep the bounds and leave the country. It is too early to pass judgment on his course.

But the really typical Associated Press men are those whose names you never see at all, men who do not write dispatches themselves, but who decide what stories to cover, who assign the writers, who instruct them what to emphasize and what to play down. The "bureau manager," so-called, has little glamour, and though he may not make as big an income as the celebrity, his job does not depend on the whims of the public or the decision of some executive. For the bureau manager is an executive himself and hopes, someday, to hold an important position in the head office. The Associated Press has such a man in the person of John Lloyd who used to head the Paris bureau and followed the government to Vichy. Lloyd had worked as an Associated Press correspondent in Buenos Aires and then in Moscow. Cool, heady, a first-rate reporter in his own right, he has chosen not to exploit his name in a "by-line" but has preferred to work for a different kind of reward in the executive field. Again and again, especially in press-association news, it is not the man who writes the news who gives us the impressions we receive. It is the

91

bureau manager who tells the correspondent how to put his story together.

Webb Miller, general European manager of the United Press, who was killed by a train during a London blackout early in 1940, combined the duties of bureau manager with the duties of a reporter. He divided his time between directing the work of others and covering important assignments himself. His autobiography, *I Found No Peace*, published in 1936, gives a better idea than any of the other newspaper books what it is like to be a newspaperman. Miller was born on a farm in Michigan. He learned the newspaper business in Chicago shortly before the last war. He came to Europe during the last war and worked there the rest of his life. He married an English wife, but was one of the few American correspondents abroad who always kept a purely American point of view. His roots in the Midwestern soil may account for this, or again it may be that his executive duties prevented him from falling into the conventional crusading pattern.

Since Webb Miller's death, Edward W. Beattie, Jr., has been covering most of the bigger European stories for the United Press. A tall, burly American who looks as Scotch as his name, Beattie joined the United Press when he was graduated from Yale, and one of his first dispatches to attract attention was a masterly coverage of the rout of the bonus army in 1932. The next year he went to Europe and since then has covered many important assignments all over the world. He has written war news from Ethiopia and the Far East. He saw German troops take over Vienna and Prague. He got through the first reports of the Nazi air bombardment of Warsaw. At thirty-two he is one of the most experienced reporters in the business and—like Webb Miller—he does not belong to the crusading school of journalism.

Several other United Press correspondents deserve special mention. Wallace Carroll, head of the London bureau, is rated one of the best agency men in Europe. Quiet, accurate, industrious, a good judge of situations, vaguely liberal but without strong political convictions, Carroll has a long background in Europe. Although still in his middle thirties he has covered Geneva and Paris as well as London for the United Press. When you are reading one of his dispatches—and it is almost certain to carry his by-line—you are getting the point of view of a man whose news strategy resembles the military strategy of the Confederacy's General Johnston who believed in "getting their fustest with the mostest." In C. T. Hallinan, the London bureau of the United Press has the ablest writer on British financial and economic affairs. Older than Carroll, Hallinan preserves an Irish-American's suspicions of British high finance.

It is also likely that you have seen the name of Reynolds Packard on United Press dispatches from abroad. Packard is the embodiment of the Hollywood foreign correspondent. He has an overriding ambition to scoop the Associated Press—an ambition that he has gratified more than once. He prides himself on not being a crusader and has remained more American than European. He used to cherish literary ambitions and spent six months in the South Seas writing a book called *Mad About Women* which got published in Paris. A United Press bureau chief once threatened to fire him because he grew a beard. His wife, Eleanor Packard, helps him and often signs her own stories. Some people call her a more dependable correspondent than her husband.

The tendency of the Associated Press in its foreign news is to give wide authority to the bureau manager. Most of the AP correspondents abroad therefore play an anonymous role. The tendency of the United Press is to lay more emphasis on the individual correspondent. The United Press is also more inclined to leave one man in one place until he becomes an expert. The Associated Press shuffles its people about more frequently.

It is quite in keeping with the character of Hearst's International News Service that it should have in its employ the two biggest names among the American newspapermen abroad—Karl H. Von Wiegand and H. R. Knickerbocker. Unquestionably, Von Wiegand has the most remarkable contacts of any American journalist in Europe. He first came to Europe in 1911 for the United Press and got bawled out by Roy Howard in July, 1914, for spending too much money on a cable that warned of approaching war. Von Wiegand quickly made friends among the German military aristocracy and it was through an interview of his with Admiral von Tirpitz that the world first learned of Germany's plans for unrestricted submarine warfare. His work as a war correspondent attracted the attention of Hearst who bought him away from the United Press and who has kept him on his payroll ever since. Although Von Wiegand has had several exclusive interviews with Hitler, his closest contacts lie with members of the old regime, the army, and the nobility.

Von Wiegand is the last survivor of a school of journalism that is no more. When he comes to a city, he does not request interviews; he is sent for and his advice is sought. Colonel House thought highly of him during the last war. French statesmen pumped him for information about Germany on the verge of this one. Von Wiegand himself is of German extraction but he was born and brought up in the United States. He is a man of intense pride and enormous personal courage: a few years ago doctors despaired of his sight, but he cured himself though he still has to wear extremely thick glasses and reads with some difficulty. In his interviews he makes frequent use of the first person singular—not so much to dramatize himself as to give authority.

If Von Wiegand is the embodiment of the old-fashioned European journalist, H. R. Knickerbocker is the embodiment of the old-fashioned American journalist. Von Wiegand, close to seventy, is old enough to be Knickerbocker's father, and their prima-donna temperaments frequently lead to friction, the more so as Von Wiegand is

95

chiefly interested in trying to understand the Nazis whereas Knickerbocker is chiefly interested in trying to stop them. In the United States the following of both these men is limited principally to readers of the Hearst press. In Europe, no other American journalists command such prestige.

Ten years ago, as general European correspondent for the *Philadelphia Public Ledger*, H. R. Knickerbocker won the Pulitzer Prize for an excellent series of articles on Russia. Although these articles carried the title "The Red Trade Menace" they gave an objective description of Russian conditions when the first Five-Year Plan was just getting under way. Knickerbocker followed this up with another series on Germany, but by that time he had become a celebrity and went over to Hearst. Since the early 1930's he has therefore drifted farther and farther away from the big assignments that made his reputation and has gone in more and more for sensationalism and prophecy. Thus, in May, 1938, when Von Wiegand was prophesying no war, Knickerbocker saw war that spring. In the summer of 1939 he wrote a series of articles for the *Petit Parisien* warning the French of the horrible fate in store for them if they did not resist the Nazis. And when the war broke out, it was Knickerbocker who sponsored the story about the millions of dollars that the big Nazi leaders were supposed to have deposited abroad. Yet in spite of having committed perhaps more than his share of mistakes, Knickerbocker remains one of the most exciting reporters in the business. A redheaded Texan he has never become Europeanized. But perhaps that's because he has never stayed in one place long enough to become identified with it anyway.

More important today than the personality of the correspondent or the organization for which he works is the city from which he writes. Every European capital—belligerent and neutral—imposes so many restrictions that an unknown quantity of news simply never gets through. Conditions change from day to day, but to give you something to go on I am listing some of the chief foreign news centers and describing briefly the character of the news you can expect to get from each.

London. The British capital remains not only the most important but the freest news center outside the United States. The British press is permitted to criticize the conduct of the war and, since Churchill became Prime Minister, appears to have received official encouragement to lambaste the appeasers who conducted the war until the month of May. Defeatist opinion is of course restrained, but there is a sharp distinction between the news stories and the photographs that are permitted to reach the outer world. The British themselves know how much damage their country has suffered, therefore the government does not need to suppress photographs showing the destruction wrought by the Germans. Furthermore, these photographs create sympathy in the United States, especially if they appear in conjunction with news stories that describe—perhaps overoptimistically—the high morale of the people. All censors have their quirks; the British censors, being British, are more eccentric than most. But, being British, they are tolerant and reasonable, and in the long run the news from London gives an extraordinarily fair and accurate picture of what is really happening in the British Isles.

Berlin. When Oswald Garrison Villard visited Germany a few months after the war broke out, officials told him that Germany had no censorship because it was a totalitarian country, not a democracy. This statement was not so absurd as it sounds. The Germans have their own press under complete control and any German caught reading a foreign publication or listening to a foreign radio broadcast may suffer the death penalty. Therefore, the Germans allow foreign correspondents a surprising amount of freedom. Radio scripts are carefully censored but newspaper dispatches go through automatically. Correspondents of course know that they must work within certain limits, and when they overstep the bounds—out they go. But they are not requested to leave the country until after the offending dispatch has reached the outer world. This does not mean that correspondents in Germany can tell anything like the whole truth, but it does mean that the news from Germany does not take the form of straight government releases, rewritten for foreign consumption by the foreign correspondents on duty there. Military secrets are of course closely guarded—in Germany and everywhere else. There are only occasional references to popular morale. Discussion of Soviet-German relations is all but taboo, and no aspersions can be cast at the Rome-Berlin Axis. No real news at all reaches the outer world from Poland, Czechoslovakia, and other occupied regions.

Moscow. Here the censorship is complete. Literally nothing comes out of the Soviet Union except straight government propaganda. Even translations from the Russian press are heavily censored.

Rome. The Italian press, especially the Vatican publications, enjoy just a little more freedom and express just a few more opinions than the German press. Mussolini's dictatorship has never operated as rigidly and efficiently as the German dictatorship. Of course, dispatches from Italy are more heavily censored than those from England, but the real pay-off on news from Italy is that there just isn't much of it. Remember that Italy is not a first-rate, major power, and therefore less news originates there than in the larger countries.

Paris. News from the former French capital passes through the Berlin censorship and is therefore more closely scrutinized before it goes abroad than news originating in Berlin. Because of changing conditions in unoccupied France, no generalizations are likely to hold good for more than a week or two.

Tokyo. Conditions in Japan are changing so fast that it is difficult to generalize about the censorship. The Japanese press itself still retains some diversity, and samples of

99

various schools of opinion can reach the outer world. There is an army party in Japan which favors expansion on the Asiatic mainland. There is a navy party which wants to expand overseas, especially in the direction of the East Indies. There are radical young army officers who favor virtual socialization of wealth but who would of course retain the Mikado. And there is big business which is not too keen on war. But the government of Prince Konoye has curbed all these groups and has tried to set up a totalitarian type of state in which big business will play some part, in which the army and navy will come into play, and in which the hotheaded young officers will be given more authority. More than ever since Japan joined the Axis, the trend is toward a form of national socialism and toward military and naval expansion. Under these circumstances, news from Japan will naturally be subject to increasingly severe censorship that is chiefly concerned with convincing the world of Japan's invincible power and unshakable determination to assert itself.

All these generalizations are subject to change without notice. When the German troops swept across the Low Countries and France, the news from the German High Command proved a lot more accurate than the news from the British and the French. But when the German invasion of Britain ran into some snags, the British reports of the air battles proved more accurate than the German reports. Indeed, one way to get at the truth about any military campaign is to give greater credence to the reports from the side that is having the better of it at the moment. This, of course, cannot be determined at once, but in the light of what has happened on half a dozen different battle fronts, we are beginning to be able to size things up more intelligently than we could a year ago. To put it in a nutshell: a confident, winning country can afford to let the truth be known; a country in difficulties at home or abroad clamps down more severely on the news.

Much of our news now comes from the smaller capitals —Lisbon, Stockholm, Berne, Sofia, Bucharest, Belgrade, Budapest. Again, a changing situation makes generalization impossible, but it is safe to say that the censorship in the smaller neutral nations does not bear down quite so heavily as it does in the larger nations—belligerent or neutral. As for the Far East from which we shall be getting more and more news, Shanghai remains relatively free. News from Australia and New Zealand is also largely uncensored. India, on the other hand, lives under a censorship that is only slightly less severe than the censorship of a German-occupied territory. And one final tip: read with the utmost skepticism anything from the Balkans.

7

TWO GREAT FOREIGN SERVICES

☆ ☆ ☆ ☆ ☆

MOST OF the news we get from abroad comes from three press associations and from the special correspondents of half a dozen individual newspapers that maintain foreign services of their own. During the past ten years, however, even those few American newspapers that have kept up independent foreign services have had to curtail their operations, and the outbreak of war has accelerated the process. In consequence, only two newspapers—*The New York Times* and the *Chicago Daily News*—have a really comprehensive foreign coverage of their own. Indeed, as the supply of foreign correspondence has gradually declined, the demand for better foreign coverage has increased.

Only *The New York Times* and the *Chicago Daily News* have risen to the occasion. Both papers now have large enough staffs of correspondents abroad and have syndicated the work of these correspondents through enough different newspapers in the United States to deserve as much attention as the press associations. Of course, the work of their correspondents is not so widely read as the work of the press-association correspondents. On the other hand, the setup of the two papers is such that each one offers a more distinctive interpretation of foreign news than you can find anywhere else.

This is especially true of *The New York Times* which has become not only the most important American newspaper in its own right but which covers the news more thoroughly in many ways than the press associations themselves. The *Times* owes its superiority to the fact that, large as it is, it does not suffer from the organizational curse of bigness. The Associated Press and the United Press have become world-wide empires with all those officials and hierarchies that empires breed. *The New York Times*, on the other hand, remains a monument to the genius of Adolph S. Ochs, and to this day, members of his family still control the paper. His son-in-law, Arthur Hays Sulzberger, is president of the New York Times Company; his wife, the former Iphigene Ochs, is a fellow director; so is Colonel Julius Ochs Adler, Mrs. Sulzberger's first cousin. There are only two other directors—Godfrey Nelson and Hoyt Miller—and the only "interlocking directorate" is that with the Spruce Falls Power & Paper Company, Ltd., of Toronto, from which the *Times* gets its paper. The *Times* represents, of course, the point of view of New York high finance, not because the directors have any commitments or obligations in that direction but because that is the world in which they live, move, and have their being. What William Allen White once wrote about

103

the editor of any American newspaper applies to the owners and editors of *The New York Times* as much as it does to the corresponding figures on the least important paper in the land:

"I know of no editor so high that his mind is not affected by his industrial environment. The fact that he lives in daily contact with the rich people of his community, whether the community be large or small, that he gangs with them at the country clubs, eats with them at the leading hotels, and indeed prays with what might be called a plutocratic congregation, colors his views and he sees things as his friends and associates see them." The heirs to Adolph Ochs "pray," it is true, in a reformed synagogue rather than a Protestant or a Catholic church. But the religious and racial factor in cosmopolitan New York plays an insignificant part as compared with social and economic ties which crisscross the religious and racial ones. And the predominant point of view of the predominant people of New York is international in general and pro-British in particular.

This point of view is reflected not only on the *Times* editorial page but in its news columns; indeed, *The New York Times* is the only American newspaper that employs a substantial number of British subjects in key positions abroad. These include Hugh Byas, head of the Tokyo bureau, G. E. R. Gedye, former bureau chief in Moscow, and P. J. Philip, former bureau chief in Paris. Another British subject, Frederick T. Birchall, had a wandering assignment in Europe for many years and at the early part of the present war moved to Canada. The *Times* also uses political articles by Sir Arthur Willert, former head of the press department of the British Foreign Office, and by a White Russian, V. Poliakov, who signs himself "Augur" and who has long been the unofficial spokesman for an inner clique of Tory Die-Hards. Captain B. H. Liddell Hart writes on military strategy and the recently deceased Hector C. Bywater used to discuss naval affairs. Since the inception of the present war, however, the *Times* has leaned almost entirely on Hanson W. Baldwin, an Annapolis graduate, as its military and naval expert.

One of the healthiest developments under the Sulzberger regime has been the gradual replacement of Britishers by Americans in the *Times* foreign service. If Von Wiegand and Knickerbocker embody two contrasting forms of the old-fashioned type of foreign correspondent, Otto D. Tolischus represents the new type at its very best. He headed the Berlin bureau of *The New York Times* from 1933 to the spring of 1940, when the Nazis requested him to leave. He then set up offices in Stockholm. Tolischus does not go in for personal contact work or cultivating a romantic personality. He concentrates his attention on background, facts, and documentation. As his name indicates, he comes of Baltic stock, but he was born in the United States, attended the Columbia School of Journalism, worked on newspapers in the Middle West, and when

105

he went to Berlin for the *Times* he had an excellent knowledge of European history and American journalism.

Being himself of North European extraction Tolischus gradually drove the Germans wild by beating them at their own game, and finally, in exasperation, they forced him to leave the country. What he had done was to read all the German magazines and newspapers he could lay his hands on. Then, from time to time, he would send back a dispatch correlating all that he had read into a damning picture of German intrigue. In 1937, for example, he described with complete footnotes the Nazi network abroad, but the German authorities let him stay on when he proved to them that he had pieced his whole story together from exclusively Nazi sources. Tolischus is a hard-working, shy, quiet man with plenty of strong convictions which he has known how to harness to his newspaper job. His record shows that the great reporter can still report and carry a torch at the same time.

Raymond Daniell who took over the London office of *The New York Times* just about the time the war broke out is another outstanding newspaperman of the new school. Tolischus is a little over forty; Daniell is a little under. Daniell is perhaps the better leg man; Tolischus the better researcher. Daniell used to cover the great American hinterland and knew Huey Long well. A liberal in his political views, he almost was run out of Alabama for his fearless handling of the second trial of the Scottsboro boys. Early in 1939 he went to Mexico to replace

106

Frank Kluckhohn whom the Mexican government had ejected. Daniell is sympathetic to the British cause, but because he has not lost his American perspective, he presents the British case more effectively to American readers than the more ardent Anglophiles, like Harold Callendar, on the *Times* staff.

Herbert Matthews, who covered the Ethiopian and Spanish wars for the *Times* and who became head of the Rome bureau in 1939, is another first-rate man. A gangling, serious enthusiast, he easily identifies himself with the people among whom he is working. Thus, he was pro-Italian in Ethiopia, pro-Loyalist in Spain. Absolutely fearless, he says his easygoing temperament needs a bombing to bring it up to normal excitability. He has managed to get more information past the Italian censor than any other newspaperman in Rome and now has an excellent general knowledge of European politics, especially in the Mediterranean region.

Two of the last three *Times* correspondents in Moscow have been Englishmen—Walter Duranty and G. E. R. Gedye—and both of them prefer the red to the old-school tie. Duranty headed the *Times* bureau in Moscow from 1922 to 1935 and spotted Stalin as the coming man before Lenin died. He always cultivated close relations with the Kremlin, and some people credit him with having played a considerable part in gaining American recognition for the USSR. In any case, his book, *I Write As I Please*, won a lot of friends and influenced a lot of people to take a more sympathetic view of Stalin's Russia. Anti-Communists call Duranty a "Stalinist," yet when he began prophesying the Nazi-Soviet Pact immediately after Munich, orthodox comrades denounced him as a cynic and worse. He justified—or at any rate rationalized—the Moscow trials, and as late as June, 1940, he warned the American readers of his dispatches not to let their country get involved in the European war. Duranty often writes erratically; he always exploits his own strong personality; but even on an off day he writes more penetratingly than most of the smoother performers. He still contributes sporadic dispatches to the *Times* from Central and Eastern Europe and they are always worth reading.

Harold Denny, a first-rate American reporter who had covered the Ethiopian war, succeeded Duranty in Moscow. He arrived at a difficult period—the purges were just beginning—and what sympathy he had for the Soviet experiment soon evaporated. In 1939, he left in a state of considerable disillusionment and was succeeded by the starry-eyed G. E. R. Gedye who had represented the conservative *Daily Telegraph* of London in Central Europe and had headed *The New York Times* Vienna bureau until Hitler took over Austria. From Vienna Gedye went to Prague where he became strongly anti-Chamberlain, passionately pro-Czech, and decidedly friendly to the Soviet Union. He believed in Moscow's protestations of devotion to the principle of collective security, and when he went to Moscow after the Germans occupied Prague in March, 1939, he said it would be a relief to go to a city that the Germans would not take over. Six months later, von Ribbentrop arrived at the Kremlin to sign the Nazi-Soviet Pact.

At this point the scales began to fall from Gedye's eyes. He rationalized the pact in his dispatches just as Duranty rationalized the Moscow trials, but the Finnish war extended his education. When the Russians instituted a complete censorship on January 1, 1940, Gedye perceived that he could get nothing more from Russia for an indefinite period, but he remained on the job until September. Nevertheless, when he did leave the country and "told all," it was not an embittered or even a disillusioned story that he related. He explained Stalin's policy solely in terms of Russian weakness and by no means ruled out the possibility of Anglo-Soviet collaboration. He saw nothing but friction ahead for Germany and Russia. Gedye is one of the best writers on any newspaper, and his *Betrayal in Central Europe*, a book about the collapse of Austria, is a minor classic in its field. Its criticism of Neville Chamberlain lost the author his job on the *Daily Telegraph*.

Percy J. Philip belongs to the vanishing generation of *Times* correspondents and has little in common with his fellow Britons, Duranty and Gedye. As head of the Paris bureau for many years he was the power behind the scenes of the influential Anglo-American Press Club. A friend of Bonnet and the appeasers, anti-Loyalist in Spain, anti-Popular Front in France, a politician among newspapermen and a newspaperman among politicians, he finds himself in a curious position since the fall of France. For Philip is a British subject, Scottish by birth and Tory by conviction. Thus he has lived to see his native land betrayed by the traitors whose congenial political views blinded him to their other shortcomings.

Since the collapse of France, G. H. Archambault has taken over at Vichy the job Philip used to do in Paris. Because Archambault has not attacked the Pétain regime, he has been accused of pro-Fascist sympathies. Actually he has no strong political attachments, but of course he cannot criticize things as they are and send out any material at all. In other words, he works under the same handicaps and restrictions as the *Times* men in Berlin, Rome, or any other country under totalitarian rule. Archambault himself is a Frenchman of sixty who received his education in England and married an English wife. He edited the *Paris Herald* for James Gordon Bennett and is wildly, rabidly pro-American. Before the collapse, he abused all the French bureaucrats, regardless of their political affiliations, and concentrated his energies on getting the news to the outside world. His wings have of course been clipped, but he does the best he can.

Hugh Byas, head of *The New York Times* bureau in Tokyo, also represents *The Times* of London in the Japanese capital. He knows the Far East well, has lived there for a quarter of a century, and makes a point of writing different dispatches for his two papers. From the time

110

Roosevelt entered the White House until the outbreak of the Second World War, Anglo-American policy in the Far East followed the line of "parallel action." But the immediate German menace led the British to revert for a while to the policy of Far Eastern appeasement that they had followed in 1933. It was then that Sir John Simon as Foreign Secretary refused to support Secretary Stimson's protest to Japan concerning the invasion of Manchuria, thus leaving the United States the only major power that supported the principle of the Open Door in China. By the fall of 1940, however, the position of Great Britain had become so very much worse and the Dominions of Australia and New Zealand had become so completely dependent on American naval protection, especially after Japan joined the Axis, that "parallel action" became the order of the day. Indeed, it looked as if the United States might have to take over almost the entire job of upholding the *status quo* in the Far East. All of which suited Mr. Byas' book, for like many Englishmen who have lived long in the Far East he believes that the United States and England must stand together. Nor is he too much of a stickler about who will become the senior partner in the firm.

Thus *The New York Times* provides an extensive foreign service with a mild but diminishing British flavor. Because the *Chicago Daily News* prides itself on the hundred per cent Americanism of its reporters abroad, they have no reluctance about editorializing their dispatches.

111

Before the war broke out, the *Chicago Daily News* foreign service was gradually substituting exhortation for straight reporting, until by the fall of 1940 several members of its staff had transformed themselves from newspapermen into propaganda agents for American intervention in Europe's war.

A strange collection of bedfellows brought about this state of affairs. The *Chicago Daily News* staff in Europe has long been headed by Edgar Ansel Mowrer, a thorough liberal and America's foremost Hitler hater abroad. On this side, however, the *Chicago Daily News* is owned by one of our greatest living jingoes—Colonel Frank Knox— and a group of conservative big businessmen. These men not only speak with the voice of American big business; they see salvation for America in a streamlined program of expansion, imperialism, and manifest destiny.

Colonel Knox himself campaigned with Teddy Roosevelt as a Rough Rider and still echoes the slogans of the Spanish-American War. He learned the newspaper business working for Hearst, but in 1931 he left an important executive position in the Hearst organization to go in for himself with the *Chicago Daily News*. According to Raymond Gram Swing who once worked for Knox, the Colonel has always wanted "to round out his life with one great achievement. He dreamed of making it [the *Chicago Daily News*] the best newspaper in the English-speaking world, best in style, information, opinion, and appearance." His foreign service, now used by twenty American newspapers, three in Canada, and one in England, costs a thousand dollars a day—and the *Chicago Daily News* does not lose money. As a smart businessman and an intelligent publisher, Colonel Knox made no objection when his star columnist, Howard Vincent O'Brien, opposed Governor Landon and himself in the 1936 presidential campaign.

The *Chicago Daily News* has closer ties with big business than *The New York Times* has. Sewell Avery, chairman of the board of Montgomery Ward and a director of half a dozen other corporations closely tied to Morgan interests, is a director of the *Chicago Daily News*. The eight other directors also hold directorships in railroads, banks, timber, and paper companies. The point, however, is not that these interests dictate *Chicago Daily News* policy. The point is that these directors—unlike the directors of the Scripps-Howard enterprises and *The New York Times*—are not exclusively or even primarily newspapermen. Rather are they business leaders who would be inclined to look upon their newspaper property as one of several holdings.

The resignation of Colonel Knox as chairman of the board of the *Chicago Daily News* when he entered the Roosevelt Cabinet is not likely to affect his newspaper's policy in the near future. The pattern he has established will almost certainly hold up for a number of years. As a newspaperman himself Colonel Knox has known how to organize this particular type of enterprise and in that respect differs, of course, from his former fellow directors, none of whom had his experience in the newspaper field. He also differs from the people who work for the paper as any employer differs from his employees. Employer and employee are at one in wanting to create a product of superior merit; they are not, however, always animated by the same motives. We have some idea of the interests and character of the men who own the *Chicago Daily News*. Now let us take a look at the people who work for it.

Edgar Ansel Mowrer, for many years head of the *Chicago Daily News* service in Europe, is one of the great journalists of our time. A brilliant talker with a gift for exaggeration, a fanatical Hitler hater and born crusader, Mowrer's militant liberalism has gradually transformed him from a reporter into a preacher. When he wrote *Germany Sets the Clock Back* shortly after Hitler came to power, he got kicked out of Berlin and since then he has campaigned up and down Europe preaching a crusade against the Nazis until the *Blitzkrieg* against France drove him over to England. His wife, an English middle-class intellectual, and his many friends among the German refugees keep his emotions boiling and he communicates his heat to the rest of his staff and to other newspapermen as well—notably to H. R. Knickerbocker.

Sometimes Mowrer's enthusiasm gets the better of him. This happened shortly before the present war when he lunched in England with a group of English newspapermen who came together to give him some pointers on the

114

local situation only to find themselves listening to his views on their country. Before the last war broke out Mowrer was studying esthetics at the Sorbonne, and there are those who say he should have become a professor. But his abilities and energies have made him a great newspaperman, almost in spite of himself. Mowrer would have made his mark whatever he did, and whatever he did a lot of people would have said he should have done something else.

When Mowrer left Europe this year, Leland Stowe became the most conspicuous if not the most important *Chicago Daily News* man on the Continent. His recent exploits have already become a saga. He had reported the Spanish Civil War for the *New York Herald Tribune* and became ardently pro-Loyalist. When the European war broke out, the *Herald Tribune* said he was too old to cover it—his white hair makes him look older than his forty-one years. He therefore packed up for Chicago, sold himself to Colonel Knox, and then covered the Finnish and the Norwegian campaigns. He scooped the world on the German Fifth Column tactics in Oslo and again on the first defeat of the British near Narvik. Since then, however, he has tended more and more to editorialize. He hit a new all-time high when he wired a long dispatch from the Balkans in late June stating that if the United States would at once send two thousand planes to Britain, Hitler would be stopped. Nevertheless, Leland Stowe is a fine newspaperman, a first-rate writer, and a universally respected citizen of the world. It is one of the curiosities of the present day that two militant liberals like himself and Mowrer should find themselves seeing eye to eye on anything with their conservative employer, Colonel Knox. But remember that Colonel Knox is a newspaperman too and it is as a newspaperman, not as a politician, that he judges the journalists in his employ.

William Stoneman, head of the *Chicago Daily News* office in London, is the third most important man in that paper's foreign service. He is a hard worker who always wanted to be a foreign correspondent and in the 1920's got himself sent to Sweden, where he received no regular salary and got paid only when he wrote a story that the home office wanted. But the Kreuger case gave him his chance and landed him a regular job on the *Daily News* foreign staff. He married a Swedish girl, went to Russia, didn't like it, also to Germany and Italy, and didn't like them either. In England he criticized the Chamberlain government for its appeasement policy and got rebuked by his boss. It was a fluke that Stowe got the chance to cover Norway because Stoneman knows the country and the language much better, but Stowe had been in Finland and Stoneman had his hands full in London. Stoneman has fewer political convictions and less personal passion about the world situation than some of his colleagues. He can write a good general political article, but he chiefly excels as a news getter.

Helen Kirkpatrick, a Smith graduate and former League

of Nations enthusiast, also works in the London office of the *Chicago Daily News*. Originally pro-British, she veered away during the appeasement period, but veered back again with the war. She helps Gordon-Lennox, diplomatic editor of the London *Daily Telegraph*, issue the *Whitehall News Letter*, one of those semiconfidential interpretations of official policy. Between them, they have access to Winston Churchill, Anthony Eden, and Sir Robert Vansittart, former permanent head of the Foreign Office who was eased out of his job by Neville Chamberlain.

Two other *Chicago Daily News* men in Europe deserve special mention. Wallace Deuel in Berlin has long understood the revolutionary aspect of National Socialism and plays it up consistently in his dispatches. Of course, he cannot openly denounce Hitler and he hasn't Mowrer's temperament anyway. But he is clearly anti-Nazi. John Whitaker, who heads the *Daily News* bureau in Rome, wrote a book about the League of Nations back in 1937. Handsome, debonair, social, he is a hard worker and a good man on digging up the news. He has excellent personal connections and enjoys scooping his competitors. His stories have more color than political interpretation, but that is almost a novelty these days.

By and large, American newspapermen abroad have a healthy sense of their importance and take pride in the fact that they are working for independent outfits. The press associations make it a policy to have no policy. *The New York Times* foreign service, which has more independence and character than any of the agencies, lays increasing stress on getting the news and is deliberately turning its back on editorializing. The worse conditions become, the more acutely the competent reporter feels his importance. There is little interference by the agency managements in the way the news is handled. They are tending to concentrate more on scoops and sensations, but their bureaucratic control makes them muscle-bound, especially by comparison with *The New York Times*.

One point deserves special mention, although it does not directly affect your understanding of the news. The Associated Press, the United Press, and all the more important foreign news services have become one of the principal instruments in spreading American influence abroad, especially in Latin America. Even before Hitler came along with his heavily subsidized Transocean press service, all the principal governments, save only that of the United States, used their news agencies as instruments of national policy. Sir Willmott Lewis, Washington correspondent of the London *Times*, once commented in this connection that all news services fall into two categories—Tass and demi-Tass. He should, however, have made an exception for the American press services which are not even "demi-Tass." Like our big radio chains which broadcast their own programs to Latin America, our press associations and newspapers have no government control at all, yet they constantly function in the national interest, both in gathering and disseminating news abroad.

118

I have not attempted here to cover every country, every news service, every type of correspondent. I have confined myself to those news agencies and newspapers, those syndicates and correspondents, with a national audience. This has left me no choice but to omit several outstanding correspondents, notably William Henry Chamberlin of the *Christian Science Monitor* and William Bird of the New York *Sun*. But since the field is growing narrower every day and the censorship is growing tighter, it is unlikely that many new sources of news will develop in the near future. Moreover, if the emphasis has been on Europe rather than on Latin America and the Far East, that is because our newspapers and the reading public seem to prefer European news. This emphasis may change, but if and when it does, you will probably see many names long associated with Europe turning up in other parts of the world.

THE CORRESPONDENTS

☆ ☆ ☆ ☆ ☆

SATIRE CAN SERVE a serious purpose here. Because the country from which a dispatch originates imposes its own type of censorship and propaganda far more strongly than the correspondent can impose his point of view, I am leading off with four dispatches on our sun, moon, and tide theme as these dispatches would come through from London, Berlin, Moscow, and Tokyo. Here goes:

LONDON, *August 3—Continued bombing attacks by German Stuka planes failed to disturb thousands of vacationing Britons as they celebrated the August bank holiday at the seaside resorts of Bournemouth and (deleted by censor). As it was low water at (deleted by censor), the beaches provided ample space for the early-afternoon crowd to watch the show and cheer the sportsmanship of the Germans who, in spite of inferior equipment, nevertheless succeeded by virtue of their superior numbers in evading the British chaser planes and wrecking several military objectives. When a German dive-bomber crashed in flames after it had set fire to an oil reservoir, the crowd stood in* bareheaded tribute to the sportsmanship of the pilot, and the band which had been playing a medley of patriotic airs burst into the strains of the Horst Wessel Song. But when it was learned that a piece of flying debris had killed a puppy, many enraged British sportsmen rushed upon the scene firing rifles, shotguns, and pistols at the hostile airmen. As the moon will not enter the new quarter until August 10, the crowd dispersed at sunset which occurred at (deleted by censor).

BERLIN, August 3—Dr. Paul Joseph Goebbels, Germany's Minister of Propaganda and Enlightenment, played host today at a sumptuous luncheon for the foreign press representatives in Berlin. The bill of fare included Polish ham, Danish cream, Norwegian herring, Dutch cheese, Swedish bread, and Brussels sprouts, washed down with French red and white wines, champagne, and Napoleon brandy. After the luncheon, Dr. Goebbels disclosed a British plot to shift the Gulf Stream and freeze out the Channel ports by making them ice-bound for eight months of the year. According to Dr. Goebbels, Jewish international scientists in the pay of the pluto-democracies have perfected a new type of high-explosive, pluto-water bomb capable of causing a gigantic eruption of the ocean floor when dropped from a sufficiently high altitude. But thanks to the superior science of Aryan Germany a secret ray has been discovered which completely nullifies the effect of the Jewish bombs, and the British have therefore failed to carry through their

121

diabolic scheme. To substantiate this statement and to show that the German authorities do not fear publication of the truth, Dr. Goebbels announced that it would be high water at Hamburg this afternoon at 5:33 o'clock, Hitler-saving time—and he didn't care who knew it.

Moscow, August 3—For the third successive week, to-day's newspapers make no mention of the war in Europe. The big news at the moment concerns an alleged plot to assassinate Stalin. Thirty Finnish Socialists and the secret agents of an unnamed foreign power are accused of having been inspired by Leon Trotsky and Norman Thomas to penetrate the city of Leningrad, disguised as Red Army colonels. According to Pravda, the plot was uncovered by a white-haired veteran of the Komsomols (Communist Youth Organization) whereas Izvestia attributes the discovery to a sixteen-year-old Old Bolshevik. In any event, the thirty Finnish Socialists confessed that they had conspired to assassinate Stalin, sabotage the First, Second, and Third Five-Year Plans as well as the Fourth, which is taking only two months to complete, thanks to the Stakhanov movement.

[The Stakhanov movement refers to the brutal speed-up system installed under the Red dictatorship in all the Russian factories. Under this system women and children, as well as men, are chained to the machines at which they work and are lashed every half-hour by Communist officials. This system was introduced in a vain attempt to forestall the complete collapse of the Soviet economy, but to date production has continued to fall. In consequence starvation is again reported, and impartial observers estimate that at least ten million victims of Communist totalitarianism will perish of hunger during the coming winter.—Editor.]

At their own request the Finns are being liquidated tomorrow, but before facing the firing squad they are all relinquishing membership in the Socialist Party and have declared their unshakable devotion to the principles of the Third (Communist) International. Tass, official Soviet news bureau, comments that the sun will continue to rise and set on the Soviet fatherland—at any rate until Stalin gives instructions to the contrary.

TOKYO, August 4 (Sunday)—Prince Konoye, creator of the New Japan and originator of the New Policy, announced today that he will restore the Old Japan by reverting to the Old Policy. The essence of the New Japan is to return to old values; the essence of the New Policy is to hark back to the old one. This combination of old and new seems paradoxical to the Western mind, but a spokesman of the Japanese Foreign Office, wearing a kimono, derby hat, sandals, horn-rim glasses, and a radiolite wrist watch, expounded the aims of the New-Old Policy of Old-New Japan and then declined to let himself be quoted or to have his remarks interpreted in any way for fear they would be misconstrued by the Western Powers who have consistently refused to understand the Japanese point of view. He did, however, declare for publication that the ultimate aim of the Empire of the Rising Sun is to become the Empire on which the sun never rises. Asked if he would let himself be quoted as to when the sun might be expected to rise on this new empire, he terminated the interview with a wave of his fan.

It would not only be impertinent to satirize the dispatches of the newer type of *New York Times* correspondent; it would be impossible. Otto Tolischus, G. E. R. Gedye, and Raymond Daniell get their stories, write them up with more freedom than the usual agency man is permitted, and that's that. But *The New York Times* still finds space for correspondents of an older school, men who specialize in the so-called "think-piece"—a cross between the interpretive type of reporting for which *The Times* of London is famous and one of the fuzzier of our own magazine articles. Here, for instance, is the way that Frederick T. Birchall, a British subject, might write up the sun, moon, and tide story:

OTTAWA, August 3—*This New World British capital provides the ideal setting in which to evaluate those cataclysmic forces which now have so much of the world in their grip. Almost two centuries have passed since British and French troops contended on Canadian soil for mastery of North America and it is three centuries since the first Brit-*

124

ish and French settlers established themselves in the wildernesses which are now crisscrossed by macadam roads and railways and over which airplanes from the United States wing their nightly way to the embarkation spots where the happy workers of this loyal member of the British Commonwealth of Nations crate them for shipment to the beleaguered mother land. That the United States has a stake in this enterprise goes without saying. Britain is today fighting America's battle, and it is only appropriate, therefore, that American planes should play their part in the forefront of the fighting.

But a factor of alarming gravity may hamper this Anglo-Saxon enterprise. Many of the airplanes being sent from Canada to the British Isles are crated in Toronto and sent from there by freight to Montreal, Halifax, or Quebec. These planes could be delivered much more rapidly if they could be flown either to Halifax, or, better yet, first to Halifax and then across the Atlantic. For the tidal currents in the St. Lawrence River, and the currents near its mouth, slow down navigation and lead to delays that may well prove fatal to the British cause. Nor is this all. With the approach of autumn the days are growing shorter. This means that fewer hours of daylight are available for flying. Under present circumstances, it is out of the question for Britain to risk the loss of planes or flyers in dangerous night flights, across the Atlantic or anywhere else. However, a high official has proposed this solution. Let the American plane companies assume responsibility for getting the planes to England, using American pilots and making the trip at their own risk. British insurance companies will, of course, be glad to issue policies covering these flights at the usual wartime rates, and it is hoped that this simple solution will meet the needs of the situation which is authoritatively described as critical.

It is a cold day that does not furnish Edgar Ansel Mowrer with some terrifying message that he hopes will awaken the American people from their disastrous torpor concerning events in Europe. For instance:

LONDON, August 3—The same sun and moon shine on Europe and America. The same tides that wash the seaboard of our Eastern states also wash the western coasts of the Old World. Between sunrise in London and sunrise in New York, between high tide at Southampton and high tide at Boston, there is but five hours' difference. And it takes less time than that for a plane to traverse the Atlantic if it flies in the stratosphere. Not only have the Germans already drawn up the plans for such a plane, they have actually built ten thousand of them and will launch them in a massed transatlantic attack the day London falls. But if the United States will send three rowboats, four pairs of oars, and a Daisy air rifle at once, Hitler can be stopped in his tracks without the loss of a single American life. If, however, we do not act now, the tide of totalitarianism will engulf us and the sun of democracy will set, never to rise again in our time.

126

8

NEWS IN BOOKS AND MAGAZINES

☆ ☆ ☆ ☆ ☆

FOUR JUST CRITICISMS can be made of the news we get in our daily papers. In the first place, newspaper publishers derive most of their revenue from advertising. While this does not greatly affect their interpretation of world news, it does not encourage a spirit of complete independence and self-reliance. In the second place, a newspaper operates on a twenty-four-hour basis and therefore cannot, in the nature of the case, take the long view on world affairs. Third, a newspaper is subject to definite space limitations and—again in the nature of the case—cannot give the full details and the complete background of every story. And fourth, a newspaper must appeal to so many different kinds of people that its selection and interpretation of the news are subject to many taboos. It might also be added that substantially the same criticisms apply to radio.

There is little that any newspaper can do to remedy this state of affairs. There is, however, something that you can do to get around it. That is to supplement your newspaper reading and radio listening with the reading of books and magazines. The book publisher, especially, does not depend on advertisers; he can let his authors take the long view and expound that view in detail; he does not have to publish only those books that give no offense to anybody. In consequence, book writers operate more freely than writers for newspapers and magazines.

The magazines—some magazines, at any rate—also operate with considerable freedom. They are subject to more rigid space limitations than books and they usually have to take more account of the sensibilities of their readers, because the wider your audience the more restrictions you impose on yourself, and magazines reach a wider audience than books. Finally, in the matter of advertising, some magazines are just as dependent on advertising as the newspapers; others could live without it but like to get the extra revenue; still others either refuse to accept or cannot get any advertising at all.

Below I have listed three groups of magazines that deal with world news. The magazines in the first group cost much more to produce than you pay for them and therefore depend primarily—as newspapers depend—on their advertisers:

> The Saturday Evening Post
> Collier's
> Liberty
> Life

The following magazines also require advertising to give you what they now do at the price you now pay, but they do not depend primarily on advertising revenue, and most of them could probably worry along after a fashion without it:

> Time
> Newsweek
> Fortune
> The Atlantic Monthly
> Harper's

The following magazines either run no advertising at all or else derive enough revenue from their subscribers or from some subsidy to be, in effect, completely independent of advertisers:

> The Reader's Digest
> The New Republic
> The Nation
> Foreign Affairs

There are, of course, other magazines that deal with world news, but the ones I have listed above include all those that devote a really substantial proportion of their space to world affairs and that have a wide enough distribution to be easily available throughout the United States.

Before analyzing some of these magazines and suggesting what you can get from each, let me make a few more points about the magazine business in general, as I did in the case of the newspaper business, and then add a few words about the book business, too. For the first step in understanding any interpretation of the news is to understand how and why that news is put before us.

A successful newspaper publisher has three jobs of almost equal importance to do. He must produce his paper, organize its many departments, and sell advertising and circulation. A successful magazine publisher must also be able to organize his enterprise and sell it to the public and perhaps to the advertiser. But straight editorial ability, the capacity to deliver the goods on the printed page, will carry a man much farther in the magazine business than in newspapers.

What is editorial ability? To put it in a nutshell, the great editor must have a limitless range of interest; he must have limitless enthusiasm; and his interests and enthusiasms must anticipate the interests and enthusiasms of the public by the length of time it takes him to get out his publication. If the great editor is also a great salesman and a great organizer, well and good, but unless he can anticipate public interest—and that means he must have wide and strong interests of his own—all the salesmanship and executive ability in the world will not take him far.

These general principles can easily be expressed in terms of dollars and cents. Any good printing establishment can produce a magazine that will knock your eye out on the newsstand. Any competent advertising agency can write a circular letter that will persuade a lot of people to enter a trial subscription. Anyone with a checkbook and a bank

130

balance can go out in the market and buy articles and stories by big-name contributors. But the trick is not to turn out a magazine that looks good. The trick is to turn out a magazine that people will want to come back for next week and next month, a magazine that people will want to resubscribe to when their first subscription expires. For magazine promotion costs run far, far ahead of magazine production costs, and promotion will pay out only over the long run. It isn't single copies and trial subscriptions that make money; it is continuing sales, whether on a newsstand or a subscription basis. And if the sales do not hold up, the advertising department hollers for more readers, the circulation department hollers for more money to get more readers, and the editorial department is left holding the bag.

In other words, editorial content and editorial content alone determines the success of a magazine. Circular letters and newsstand displays may attract readers, but only editorial content will hold them. And unless a magazine can hold readers, the cost of constantly getting new ones, especially in the face of mounting apathy and constant competition, soon becomes prohibitive. As for the advertisers, they will always prefer to spend money in a magazine that they know people like to read.

At the turn of the century, one of the great magazine editors of America promoted a kind of revolution. S. S. McClure gathered around him a group of journalists including Lincoln Steffens, Ray Stannard Baker, and Ida

Tarbell whose reports on the state of the nation earned them the title of muckraker. And it was their exposures of industrial monopoly, municipal corruption, and other abuses that gave a lot of the original impetus to the reform movement that preceded the last war.

As time went on, however, magazines became increasingly subordinate to the big advertisers, and the reform movement rather petered out anyway. George Horace Lorimer, perhaps not so great an editor as McClure but certainly a more successful one, tapped a new vein in *The Saturday Evening Post*. McClure had appealed to the reformers; Lorimer appealed to the businessman, and since the businessman was coming into his own, Lorimer prospered. The third great magazine editor of that period was Ellery Sedgwick who combined some of McClure's crusading zeal with some of Lorimer's understanding of the businessman and added to them a veneer of Yankee culture. He shot the circulation of *The Atlantic Monthly* up from less than 20,000 in 1908 to 150,000 in 1929—no astronomical figure by *Saturday Evening Post* standards. But articles in the *Atlantic*—"papers" as Ellery Sedgwick preferred to call them—frequently hit the front pages. William Z. Ripley's prophetic "Main Street or Wall Street" gave the Coolidge market a perceptible shock, and in 1928 Alfred E. Smith chose the *Atlantic* as the magazine in which to explain why he believed a Roman Catholic could serve his country in the White House without any conflict of loyalties. Moreover, during the 1920's *Harper's* paid the *Atlantic* the tribute of imitation. With Frederick Lewis Allen, a former assistant of Sedgwick's, on the staff, *Harper's* became, in effect, a New York version of the *Atlantic*.

But the 1929 crash gave all these magazines a blow from which they have not yet recovered. They continue to function, of course, but Lorimer has died, Sedgwick has retired, and Thomas Welles who reorganized *Harper's* has been replaced by Lee Hartman as chief editor. Half a dozen "quality magazines" have gone by the board or merged with others—*World's Work*, *Review of Reviews*, *Forum*, *Scribner's*, *Century*, even the ubiquitous *Literary Digest*. The younger business and professional men, the college-trained and professional women do not find their interests reflected in the magazines that flourished in the 1920's. They read many more serious nonfiction books than people did ten and twenty years ago. They spend more time with the newspapers and the radio. And when they read magazines they have three special favorites—*Time*, *Life*, and *The Reader's Digest*.

Henry R. Luce and his *Time-Life-Fortune* group of publications play such a commanding part in American life that they must have a chapter to themselves. Here I shall therefore confine myself to the other magazines dealing with world news. Of these, *The Reader's Digest* enjoys incomparably the widest influence and might, indeed, become the most powerful single publication in the country. But Mr. and Mrs. DeWitt Wallace who own and edit the magazine have always maintained a singular indifference to the kind of power that most editors seem to crave. Perhaps their avoidance of controversial, political issues accounts for the circulation of over three million copies a month that they have attracted. Perhaps it is the lack of advertising. Perhaps it is their spirit of uplift which has led them to crusade for such causes as the fight against venereal disease.

Originally, *The Reader's Digest* contained nothing but reprints from other magazines which welcomed the extra revenue the Wallaces paid for exclusive reprint privileges. This was back in the 1920's when a lot of middle-class people thought nothing of subscribing to half a dozen magazines and paying an extra quarter now and then for a copy of *The Reader's Digest* at the newsstand. But with the arrival of the depression, people began cutting down on magazines, and *The Reader's Digest* gave the cream of the crop at less cost than many of the periodicals from which it reprinted. The magazines took alarm, but it was too late. The Curtis Publishing Company which owns *The Saturday Evening Post* now refuses to let the *Digest* use any material from any of its magazines, but the *Digest* has become completely independent. The Wallaces now instigate and finance many of the articles they print, sometimes arranging for previous publication in another magazine, sometimes publishing them only in their own.

No magazine in the United States has less outside control. Not only do the Wallaces themselves own the magazine they edit; they do not have to take into account the whims of advertisers. Yet there is a little irony in the fact that a publication which has attained such complete independence uses that independence chiefly to promote general humanitarian causes of which most Americans strongly approve. During the early months of the present war, for instance, *The Reader's Digest* gave space to occasional isolationist articles by Hoover and Lindbergh; more recently it has run pieces by Dorothy Thompson and Walter Lippmann. Obviously, nobody is "using" the magazine for an ulterior political purpose; indeed, the question is whether the magazine serves any political purpose at all. All of which reflects nothing but credit on the editorial genius of DeWitt Wallace who has remained primarily interested—as most of his readers are interested—in good humor, sweetness, and light.

The Saturday Evening Post is a very different story. While *The Reader's Digest* has attracted circulation by playing down politics, *The Saturday Evening Post* antagonizes many Americans by harping too much on controversial, political issues. Along with *The Ladies' Home Journal, Country Gentleman,* the *Philadelphia Public Ledger* and the *Evening Ledger,* it is owned by members of the Curtis and Bok families. These properties are overcapitalized, but their only outside financial tie is with Drexel and Company, the Philadelphia branch of Morgan's. Thus, ownership of the Curtis publications remains, primarily, in the hands of a publishing rather than a finan-

135

cial dynasty, but it is a dynasty whose political affiliations lie with the rockribbed Pennsylvania Republicans. The *Post*'s editorials are ultraconservative, isolationist, anti-New Deal. The great preponderance of articles are in the same vein. This has narrowed the appeal of the magazine, given it a certain monotony that not only limits circulation but reduces political influence as well. There is such a thing as protesting too much.

Collier's has not made that mistake. Thomas W. Lamont used to be a director of the Crowell Company which owns *Collier's*, the *American Magazine*, and *The Woman's Home Companion*. His place has been taken by Arthur H. Lockett, a director of Lamont, Corliss and Company and of *Newsweek*. Most of the Crowell board, however, consists of men who have no other connections. William L. Chenery, editor of *Collier's*, enjoys a relatively free hand and has hired several liberals as staff writers—Kyle Crichton, John T. Flynn, Walter Davenport, Quentin Reynolds. *Collier's* depends more on staff writers than the *Post* does, yet even so it manages to get more variety into its pages because it does not hew so consistently to one political line.

Liberty, the third of the mass-circulation weeklies, was launched by the *Chicago Tribune* and the *New York Daily News*. Their failure to put it over even in the golden 1920's shows that it takes more than money to make a successful magazine. Today, *Liberty* is owned by Bernarr MacFadden who has directed its appeal to the lower-middle classes who read his true-story and confession magazines. But all the mass-circulation weeklies—*Liberty* included—publish background articles on the news and frequently scoop the newspapers with such features as the General Krivitzky series in the *Post* and Quentin Reynolds' war reporting in *Collier's*. And *Liberty* bobs up with a real surprise now and then, as when it used to run political articles by Leon Trotsky.

Although *The Atlantic Monthly* and *Harper's* both have to fight an uphill battle, both contain articles that throw light on the news behind the news. In 1939, Ellery Sedgwick sold out his controlling interest in the *Atlantic* to Richard E. Danielson, a conservative, fox-hunting Bostonian who used to own and edit jointly with Christian Herter the *Independent* and the *Sportsman*. Both Herter and Danielson married rich wives—Herter a daughter of the Pratt oil dynasty, Danielson a Deering of Chicago whose family makes agricultural machinery. Herter, a former aide to Hoover during the last war, has now gone into Republican politics. Danielson has stuck to publishing. He has retained Edward Weeks, Sedgwick's former right-hand man, as editor of the *Atlantic*, and is himself associate editor. No outside interests control the magazine, but its general tendency is naturally on the conservative side. On the war issue it has printed a large preponderance of articles favoring intervention.

Harper's offers a more balanced diet of news interpretation and deals rather more fully with foreign affairs than the *Atlantic*. The conservatism and caution of Lee Hartman and Frederick Lewis Allen are compensated, somewhat, by the third member of the editorial board, George R. Leighton, an independent liberal who knows how to get his views into the magazine. But the primary purpose of *Harper's* is to attract new authors to the highly successful book-publishing house which owns the periodical. It therefore offers a slightly more eclectic diet than the *Atlantic* which also, it is true, owns a publishing house on the side. But in the case of *Harper's*, it is the publishing house that dominates the magazine, whereas in the case of the *Atlantic*, it is the other way around.

Only the comparatively serious student of world affairs will be likely to read either *Harper's* or the *Atlantic* for the light they throw on current events, and the really serious student will go the whole hog and subscribe to *Foreign Affairs*. This quarterly review, issued by the Council on Foreign Relations and edited by Hamilton Fish Armstrong, prints too many articles by stuffed shirts, but it does cover its field and every issue contains three or four original contributions to modern history. *The Living Age*, with its monthly collection of reprints and translations from the foreign press, presents background material not available elsewhere, but war, censorship, and the rapid pace of events have made its task increasingly difficult. *Events*, edited by Spencer Brodney, former editor of *Current History*, relies almost entirely on college professors who summarize the month's news. As for *Current History*, it has gone through so many changes of management since *The New York Times* dropped it five years ago that it is difficult to characterize at any given moment.

The approach of the Second World War gave one of America's two liberal weeklies an attack of the blind staggers; the outbreak of the Second World War had the same effect on the other. Even before its seventy-fifth birthday had arrived in the spring of 1940, *The Nation* had gone into a grievous decline. The magazine that had been owned and edited by the incorruptible Oswald Garrison Villard throughout the 1920's recently came into the possession of one of Mr. Villard's eager assistants, Miss Freda Kirchwey. *The Nation* always ran at a deficit; under Miss Kirchwey's management it has not only suffered from a lack of funds, it has suffered from the lack of any firm, directing intelligence. The one function that *The Nation* is supremely equipped to perform is a critical function; under Miss Kirchwey's editorship it plumped for the doctrine of collective security in foreign affairs and, in domestic matters, supported the New Deal as uncritically as a delegate to the Democratic National Convention. The point is not that collective security or the New Deal were "wrong"; the point is that *The Nation* dropped its consistently critical attitude and championed causes that other publications preached more effectively. Thus it exchanged its one distinctive characteristic for exactly nothing at all.

The New Republic did not support the war quite as soon

as *The Nation*. Until the German invasion of the Low Countries it steadily criticized Roosevelt's foreign policy from the Left. Except in John T. Flynn's column, it had supported the New Deal, but the fall of France and the threat to Britain led its editors to apologize for their negligence in not having recognized sooner what Walter Lippmann, Dorothy Thompson, and Walter Winchell had been pointing out to a somewhat larger public for some time—the threat of Hitler to the American way of life. *The New Republic* did, however, uphold the principles of liberalism more courageously than *The Nation*. Whereas *The Nation* dropped Oswald Garrison Villard's antiwar column at the time of the invasion of the Low Countries, *The New Republic* retained John T. Flynn who stuck to his pacifist guns. But what really distinguishes Flynn from other liberals is not his opposition to the war—even Maxwell Stewart of *The Nation* opposed conscription—what distinguishes Flynn from his fellow liberals is that he does not spend his life in an ivory tower or in the company of other liberals. Instead, he makes it his business to see representative Americans in every walk of life.

Neither *The New Republic* nor *The Nation* operates at a profit; both need "angels" to keep them in business. Mr. Villard used to finance *The Nation*. Since Miss Kirchwey took over, there has been no substantial fortune behind the magazine. *The New Republic* operates on a fund set up by the widow of Willard Straight. Mrs. Straight is now married to an Englishman named Elmhurst, and the so-called "Elmhurst Fund" now maintains several magazines including *The New Republic* and *Asia*. There has been no discernible sign of British influence on *New Republic* policy; on the contrary. But any endowed institution shelters the people who work for it from some of the harsher realities of our competitive society. This is not to cast aspersions on any endowed institution. To be able to work in an atmosphere not dominated by considerations of profit is a rare boon. It also breeds objective minds and independent spirits. But in a period when dividends are declining and taxation is increasing, the endowed institution may find itself in trouble. The very uncertainty of its future may well disturb the philosophic calm of those whom it has protected from the slings and arrows of outrageous fortune.

Nevertheless, *The New Republic* and *The Nation* remain the favorite reading matter of the Washington correspondents who find in the pages of these liberal weeklies an atmosphere of relatively free criticism such as their own papers seldom tolerate. Moreover, after *The New Republic* and *The Nation* recovered from the invasion of the Low Countries, the fall of France, and the uproar they and the rest of the liberals raised yelling for military conscription, they began to get their bearings. They lit into Lindbergh with all the fury of a journalistic hack denouncing the man-eating shark. And the flailing arms of Wendell Willkie affected them as the sight of a windmill affected Don Quixote. Since Hoover left the White

House, American liberals have had nobody to crusade against at home. They could not get worked up about Landon, but the emergence of Willkie acted upon them just like a shot in the arm. It is therefore perhaps unfortunate that by 1941 the latest bugaboo of the liberals is almost certain to be either forgiven or forgotten.

One of the few liberal journals that has kept its head has been *Common Sense*. This monthly publication is edited by Alfred Bingham, maverick son of ex-Senator Hiram Bingham of Connecticut, and the poet, Selden Rodman. These two young men, both graduates of Yale, have enough money of their own and can raise enough from friends to maintain their modest publication at a modest loss. None of our liberal periodicals has more distinguished contributors and when they write for *Common Sense* they write as they please. Bingham has written a book entitled *The United States of Europe* and has edged farther and farther away from the isolationist views he once held. Rodman has remained leery of the war. But their chief virtue is that neither of them has acquired that air of priggish infallibility that so many liberals cultivate. Their weakness, it must be frankly admitted, is that for all their intelligence, modesty, and good will they have somehow failed to make their magazine as interesting as it should be.

But the caution of the daily papers and the refusal of the liberals to quit their ivory towers have opened up a new field of journalism. In the April, 1940, issue of *Harper's* Ferdinand Lundberg had an article about the

growing importance of the news letter—weekly, fortnightly, and monthly. Porter Sargent, who issues an informal multigraphed bulletin of his own, estimates that
there are now as many as five hundred of these news letters
in the United States and says that he has a hundred different ones in his files. But Mr. Lundberg is probably correct
when he estimates that three of the news letters have
ninety per cent of the circulation—the Whaley-Eaton
Service, the Kiplinger Washington Letter, and the Business and Legislative Report of the Research Institute of
America. The various Whaley-Eaton Services, of which
there are several, pioneered in the field. They go to six or
seven thousand people a week, sell for $25 to $30 a year,
and cover Washington news, foreign news, and the Far
East. The Kiplinger Letter costs $18 a year and reaches
40,000 people a week. Kiplinger himself used to cover the
United States Treasury for the Associated Press. He started
his letter in 1921. Whaley and Eaton are two lawyers who
went into the newspaper business and then started their
information service in 1918. Kiplinger brings inside Washington stuff to businessmen; Whaley-Eaton specializes in
facts and little-known background material.

The Business and Legislation Report is a child of the
New Deal. Published in New York City, it tells businessmen how New Deal legislation will affect them. Since the
Munich Conference, it has also gone in heavily for information on how the war and the government's war plans
will affect American business. It is largely economic and

statistical, but its editors boast they called the turn correctly on every major decision the Supreme Court has made since Roosevelt entered the White House.

All these letters provide definite services and all of them are frankly commercial enterprises. Franklyn Roudybush publishes a diplomatic letter from Washington, "Week by Week." It is staffed by diplomatic, army, and naval experts and has a good record of forecasting events abroad. The International Statistical Bureau of New York also has a fortnightly foreign letter, with the emphasis on economics. Neither of these two has any ax to grind and both have done a better job of analysis and prophecy than the newspapers, magazines, or radio. Then there are a host of propaganda news letters. George Seldes claims a circulation of 30,000 for a fortnightly printed letter "In Fact," which has never deviated from the line of the Communist Party. Mr. Seldes, who is not a Communist himself, has Bruce Minton, formerly of the New Masses, as his assistant. Their publication is strongly antiwar; it almost always contains some sensational, personal item of news or gossip; it has the authentic Seldes flavor, a combination of energy, bitterness, and assurance.

"Uncensored," a multigraphed weekly letter is edited in New York by Sidney Hertzberg, a member of the Socialist Party who has worked on The New York Times and on Time. F. C. Hanighen collects its Washington news. Less sensational than "In Fact," "Uncensored" also specializes in debunking the war from the anti-Fascist point of view. Also antiwar but pro-Fascist—pro-American Fascist, that is—is Lawrence Dennis' "Weekly Foreign Letter." Dennis writes brilliantly, reads widely, knows diplomacy and finance from the inside, but too often falls victim to his own brilliance as a phrase-maker and a fatal weakness for oversimplification. From the strictly anti-Fascist side comes "The Hour," backed by Wythe Williams, Hendrik Willem van Loon, and other celebrities. It exposes Fascist and Nazi tendencies everywhere—in the United States and abroad. "Inside Germany Reports," issued monthly by the American Friends of German Freedom, used to provide by far the best inside information on Germany available anywhere. It got its information from an underground group connected with the Socialist Party in the United States, but the defeat of France destroyed—at least temporarily—its channels of communication.

The commercial services flourish because they really deliver the goods, and they deliver the goods because they know what their readers want and then go out and get it. The Kiplinger and Whaley-Eaton people, for instance, never attend press conferences. They get all their information and impressions from talking to government officials. Frequently, too, people come to them with information that they want made known. None of these services depends on advertisers; the commercial ones do not even need to tell their readers what the readers want to hear. They can speak quite frankly but cannot afford to make too many mistakes. The propaganda news letters, on the other hand, peddle dope to addicts. They, too, must have some respect for accuracy, but they must not do violence to the prejudices of their readers or put their own cause in a bad light.

The most useful propaganda news letters are those that specialize in some one field. Thus, the "Inside Germany Reports" really do gather authentic information from sources that the ordinary newspaper does not reach. "In Fact," on the other hand, proceeds on the theory that vested interests of one kind or another twist and suppress news of every description. It therefore covers all kinds of news and gives what is supposed to be the lowdown on everything from international affairs to labor relations. Obviously, a publication staffed by two or three people cannot do more than pick up an occasional loose ball. Moreover, a crusading service of this kind is prone to stack the cards in favor of radicalism just as the orthodox press stacks the cards in favor of conservatism. In reading any propaganda news service it is therefore just as well to make the same allowances you would make in reading any other publication.

I have already remarked that books offer the only existing medium for the relatively free communication of ideas. Let me elaborate just a little. The book-publishing business is not a big-money business. There are not half a dozen writers in America who make a good living exclusively by writing books. Successful book writers can always make more money by working other more lucrative fields

—and most of them do. Unsuccessful book writers have to seek other sources of revenue and must regard their book writing as purely a side line. Although I know of no philanthropist who has ever set up a fund to support aged and indigent book publishers, it is also a fact that the big publishing fortunes lie in other fields. Inescapably, the book publisher is a "little businessman"; the American people don't spend enough money on books to enable anybody to become a multimillionaire selling them. On the other hand, because book publishing is not "big business" the various publishing firms have resisted the tendency to form mergers. The book business thus remains a diversified one in a period of combination and conformity.

In the appendix I have listed a few recent books that throw light on the news of the day. Here I have only one more suggestion to make. The Foreign Policy Association issues an excellent series of "Headline Books," bound in paper and selling at thirty-five cents each. This series gives unbiased, accurate, up-to-date coverage of the background of current events. If you are looking for something a little more solid than magazine articles but not quite so technical as *Foreign Affairs* or the books issued by the Council on Foreign Relations, this series is your dish.

9

TIME, INC.

THE MAGAZINES of S. S. McClure played a considerable role in keeping Theodore Roosevelt in the White House and in getting Woodrow Wilson there. The magazines of Henry Luce played a larger and more direct part in Wendell Willkie's presidential campaign. For it was an article by Willkie in *Fortune* that first brought him seriously to public attention as White House timber. *Time* and *Life* then built him up with a somewhat larger public, and finally Russell Davenport, *Fortune*'s managing editor, resigned his job to put Mr. Willkie across. Whatever Mr. Willkie's ultimate fate may be, he became, in 1940, a national figure who could not possibly have achieved his prominence without the *Time-Life-Fortune* build-up and backing. And if Wendell Willkie owes his prominence to *Time*, *Life*, and *Fortune*, these three magazines, in turn, owe their very existence to Henry R. Luce.

Not since the time of S. S. McClure has the United States seen a magazine genius who is Henry Luce's equal, and if his career follows its present course, he is likely to become the most powerful American magazine editor of all time. The son of a missionary in China, Luce was graduated from Yale in 1920 and when still in college told Harold Laski that he planned to start a news magazine when he was graduated. A few years later Mr. Laski saw an early issue of *Time* and assumed that somebody had got the jump on Luce because he did not believe a man of under twenty-five, without funds of his own, could launch such a publication so soon. But he soon learned different. Luce and his classmate, Briton Hadden, who died ten years ago, interested the Davison family and some other friends in putting up the money that started *Time*. It was not a lot of money, for *Time* was set up in such a way that it could pay all expenses from circulation revenue. Its own staff did all the writing; it was a simple, inexpensive printing job; it sold for 15¢ a copy, $5 a year. Of course it did go after advertising and got quite a lot. This enabled it to improve its service. But the real secret of *Time*'s success— and the success of *Life* and *Fortune*, too, for that matter— is that the controlling genius in the organization is an editorial man, not an advertising man or a circulation man. Not only does Henry Luce possess the authentic editorial instinct, he has built up an organization in which the advertising and circulation departments are always subordinate to the editorial department.

This is not to say that the success of Time, Inc., is a one-man success story. Briton Hadden set the original style of *Time*. Roy E. Larsen built up its circulation and put across "The March of Time" newsreels. Ralph Ingersoll, editor of New York's new evening tabloid *PM*, was publisher of *Fortune*. Their names, however, are only just now becoming widely known because all these men have just turned forty and their careers still lie ahead.

In *America's Sixty Families* Ferdinand Lundberg wrote: "Perhaps the most direct and significant Morgan journalistic connection is with Time, Inc." But "connection" is not "control." J. P. Morgan and Company does own a large block of stock in Time, Inc., but that is in its capacity as trustee for the Davison family who put up some of the original money. The directors of Time, Inc., also include two men with Morgan connections—Artemus Gates, president of the New York Trust Company, and William V. Griffin. Actually, however, Time, Inc., owes less to Morgan money, brains, and influence than it does to the ability of its own executives. If money and influence could alone make a successful publication, bankers would be richer than they are and the publishing world poorer.

The history of Time, Inc., is the great success story of modern American journalism. During the 1920's *Time's* circulation soon surpassed that of the quality magazines like *Review of Reviews* and *World's Work*. These reached between one and three hundred thousand readers; *Time* was approaching the half-million mark. It still had less than half the circulation of *The Literary Digest* but it made more money.

When the stock-market boom reached its peak, so did

Time, and the alert Henry Luce began seeking new fields to conquer. He and his associates had been impressed with some of the articles on business by businessmen that Sedgwick had been running in the *Atlantic;* they thought a magazine devoted entirely to the interests of the American businessman, a magazine glorifying but also criticizing American business, would go. And they launched *Fortune* just as the depression settled on the land.

Almost at once they had to depart from their original formula. They soon found that they could not get the articles they wanted from the outside and therefore did what they had done with *Time.* They set up a research staff, hired some top-notch writers, and produced the magazine in their own office. They glorified some of the tycoons of the day—Mitchell, Wiggin, and the rest—but they also printed an article that no magazine controlled by its advertising department or by big business would have touched: "Arms and the Men." This exposure of the arms traffic, far from damaging the prestige of *Fortune* with its advertisers or its readers, added immeasurably to its reputation. It is true that *Fortune* never did follow it up with the further disclosures it had promised, and you will find that story told in H. H. Railey's book, *Born Unto Trouble.* But *Fortune* did not always gape admiringly at successful businessmen after the fashion of the *American Magazine.* It went in more and more for original, analytical articles on large subjects of contemporary interest, many of them only remotely connected with business and businessmen as such, but all of them of interest to its circle of 100,000 intelligent, well-to-do readers.

All this time Luce kept his nose close to the grindstone. He was concentrating his efforts on *Fortune* and letting *Time* run on its own momentum. In consequence, its increasingly reactionary character escaped his notice. He was leaving his foreign department to Laird S. Goldsborough, who had a schoolgirl crush on Mussolini and who, after Hitler came into power, referred to Leon Blum as "spidery Jew Blum." The New Deal was riding high in the United States; the Popular Front was preparing to replace the reactionary governments of Laval and Flandin in France; the Italians were invading Ethiopia; civil war was brewing in Spain; the Baldwin government was walking the tightrope between appeasement and collective security in England. And at just this time Henry Luce divorced his first wife and married a new one—Clare Boothe Brokaw, herself a divorcee.

The former Mrs. Brokaw knew a lot of people in Washington and New York; she played around with writers, stage people, the café-society set; she wrote amusing articles for *Vanity Fair*. The hard-working puritanical Henry Luce had little time for society, café or otherwise, and although he ran two magazines he did not hobnob with the New York writing set as Mrs. Brokaw did. Now New York writers have their faults, but they have a certain tolerance or at any rate a cosmopolitanism. Exactly what happened

152

nobody on the outside can know, but following Luce's marriage to Mrs. Brokaw, *Time* stopped ridiculing the Jews; in fact, its whole style became more natural, and soon afterward Time, Inc., acquired *Life* and transformed it into a picture magazine. From then on, Henry Luce came further and further out of his shell. His wife wrote several successful plays and when Louis Kronenberger, *Time's* dramatic critic, was asked what would happen to him if he panned *Kiss the Boys Good-by* he wisecracked that it would be a case of "Kiss the Boss Good-by." Roy Larsen, general manager of all the *Time* enterprises, launched "The March of Time" newsreel and won an Academy Award the first year. And the Luce interests had already rung the bell in still another field. The newsreel carried on a technique that Larsen had first developed with his "March of Time" radio show. This feature was originally conceived as a plug for the magazine, then it was sold to a sponsor, and was finally abandoned because Time, Inc., was too busy in other directions.

Meanwhile Goldsborough was gradually eased out as foreign editor of *Time*. Robert Neville replaced him while Robert Cantwell, another liberal, went over from the book department to national affairs, replacing the more conservative John S. Martin. These changes did not cut down the circulation of *Time*; indeed, the magazine never did better. When the Second World War broke out the *Time-Life-Fortune* publications remained benevolently neutral, but in the spring of 1940 Mr. and Mrs. Luce went to Europe and got caught in the German invasion of the Low Countries. The editorial policy of *Time* promptly underwent a sea change, and on his return from Europe, Luce joined William Allen White's Committee to Defend America by Aiding the Allies. Clare Boothe—as she signs herself—stayed over a little longer and wrote some articles for *Life*. These were subsequently expanded into a book, *Europe in the Spring*, which called, in effect, for immediate American intervention. "The March of Time" issued a full-length propaganda movie in the same vein, *The Ramparts We Watch*, and Luce delivered a nation-wide broadcast on Hitler's threat to the American way of life. Simultaneously, *Time* blossomed out with its first new department in years—"National Defense."

The development of Henry Luce's personality and the history of the whole *Time-Life-Fortune* setup reflect the development and the history of the American middle class during the past twenty years. The cocky twenties were followed by a short period of struggle and despair; this, in turn, gave way to a brief humanitarian honeymoon; then, with the arrival of the Second World War, came a confused blending of panic and confidence, of liberalism and militarism. The unbroken success of Time, Inc., shows that it has always reacted spontaneously to new situations, and because Henry Luce is a great editor his publications have always reacted in the same way their readers have reacted. For the great editor does not blaze new trails; that is the function of the prophet or the reformer. The great editor reacts exactly as his public reacts. The difference is that the great editor reacts first.

The *Time-Life-Fortune* publications cannot therefore be "analyzed" in the same way that other publications can be analyzed. They are too vital for that. As for *Time's* chief rival, *Newsweek*, the only mystery there is exactly which financial group controls its policy at the moment. Selling at 10¢ a copy and $4 a year, instead of 15¢ and $5 as is the case with *Time*, *Newsweek* must have more advertising than *Time* to show a profit. But the chief difference between the two magazines arises from the fact that *Newsweek* has incurred heavy obligations in the past. It has had several managements, several editors, several policies. Whereas *Time* was a success from the start and has always been controlled by professional journalists, *Newsweek* has become more and more the property of several well-to-do families—Harrimans, Astors, Whitneys, Mellons. These families do not impose their immediate interests on *Newsweek* any more than the Morgans do on *Time*. Few financiers control their publications as directly as the muckraking journalists would have you believe—and when they do the results are disastrous to all concerned. Indeed, one weakness of *Newsweek* is that it has no firm control, no single policy. Raymond Moley's page gives it an anti-New Deal character—but who reads Raymond Moley? Its coverage of the war does not preach intervention as frankly as *Time*; perhaps that reflects the comparative absence of Morgan money, more likely the management of *Newsweek* has decided to work the other side of the street on the war issue. Which means that Henry Luce has once again gotten the jump on the competition.

☆ 10 ☆

STAND BY FOR STATION
IDENTIFICATION

☆ ☆ ☆ ☆ ☆

Close to thirty million people in the United States own radio sets, and surveys by the radio industry suggest that these sets are turned on at least three and perhaps as much as six hours a day. This means that more people own radio sets than buy daily papers and that they spend more time listening to them than they do reading—the papers or anything else. Of course, radio listeners spend only a small proportion of their time tuning in on news broadcasts, but it is also true that newspaper readers do not spend all their time reading world news. A newspaper survey conducted by Dr. George Gallup in 1932 showed only 40 per cent of all newspaper readers reading the news story under the banner headline whereas 65 per cent read the comic strips and 90 per cent looked at the news-picture page. Another Gallup survey also showed that whereas 25 per cent of all newspaper readers consulted the radio listings in 1932, the proportion had increased to 40 per cent in 1938.

While I am on the subject of figures, let me add a few more. All of them come from a documented study of radio entitled *Radio and the Printed Page*, by Paul F. Lazarsfeld, director of the Office of Radio Research at Columbia University. Dr. Lazarsfeld received a grant from the Rockefeller Foundation to survey public opinion regarding radio; he supervised a group of research workers; he also gathered the findings of other groups. And here are some of the things he discovered.

A careful study of Cincinnati radio programs and newspapers showed that in the field of foreign news and comment, radio covered about twice as many items as the newspapers, but in all the other departments of the news, the papers covered more items than the radio. Surveys of all income groups in all parts of the country show that people in rural areas and people with lower incomes and less education prefer to receive their news over the radio rather than from the newspapers. But these people devote only a small proportion of their listening time to hearing news broadcasts. City dwellers, on the other hand, and people in the higher income and higher-education brackets are more inclined to tune in on news broadcasts and on commentators when they listen to the radio at all.

Radio has greatly increased the interest in foreign news. This means that people who begin following foreign news over the radio soon start buying more newspapers. The notion that radio news bulletins and radio news commentators cut down newspaper circulation is totally false. The real rivalry between newspapers and radio lies elsewhere. It lies in the field of advertising because the national advertisers are spending more and more money on radio programs, less and less on newspaper advertising. It is the advertising competition of radio, not the competition for listeners and readers, that has caused so much grief to American newspaper—and magazine—publishers.

But it is the listener who concerns us here and in this connection it certainly seems fair to assume that the average American gets at least as much news over the radio as he does from his newspaper. This means that it is just as important to understand radio news as it is to understand newspaper news. But a great deal of this news comes from the same sources. The Associated Press, the United Press, and International News Service all issue radio news bulletins which summarize their more complete newspaper releases. Some radio commentators work on newspapers; most of them are ex-journalists; all of them get most of their news from the printed page. Newspapers own almost one quarter of all our radio stations. In other words, most of what you hear over the radio is the same news you read in your newspaper, gathered by the same people, and sometimes even commented upon by members of the working press. The one completely distinctive contribution that radio has made to news coverage is the eyewitness report of current happenings.

Nevertheless all news that comes to you by radio has certain special characteristics inherent in the radio industry, just as all the news you read in your newspaper has certain characteristics inherent in the newspaper industry.

Before analyzing specific newspapers and specific correspondents I touched on some distinguishing characteristics of the newspaper industry, and before analyzing specific radio networks and the people who talk over them, I shall therefore follow the same course and indicate some of the distinguishing characteristics of radio.

What chiefly distinguishes the radio industry from the newspaper industry or any other channel of communication is that it has some attributes of a public utility. Not only does the radio make use of the air, which belongs to the whole community; it must be regulated by the government in order to prevent innumerable stations from setting themselves up and broadcasting over the same wave lengths. In fact, the radio industry almost went to smash in the early days because the government did not regulate it. The air became such a chaos of noise that radio had to put itself under government supervision in sheer self-defense.

Under the present system of government supervision, wave lengths are assigned to individual stations. These assignments, or licenses, expire every six months and are renewed almost automatically. The Federal Communications Commission, a three-man board appointed by the President, assigns licenses and when it reaches any decision does so in "the public interest, convenience, and necessity" —these being the words used in the Act of Congress that set up the FCC in the first place. Just what "the public interest, convenience, and necessity" mean nobody quite knows, but the various stations justify their licenses by devoting a certain proportion of their time to educational and public-service programs which they put on at their own expense. They also try to avoid programs that might lead some pressure group to bring influence to bear on the FCC. And of course there are the usual laws covering libel, slander, and obscenity whereby the station, as well as the sponsor or the speaker, can be sued.

The radio industry lives in fear of the FCC and in love with the sponsors of its commercial programs. Whereas a newspaper must please only two groups of people—its readers and its advertisers—a radio station must please four—the listeners, the sponsors, the government, and the National Association of Broadcasters which is the trade association to which most of the better stations belong. Thus, newspapers and radio stations have two problems in common. Both must please the public and at the same time attract advertising. But the radio station has two additional problems. It must keep on the good side of the government and it must take responsibility for administering a code of self-regulation.

As far as pleasing the public and the advertisers is concerned, the radio industry has it all over the newspaper industry. People spend far more time listening to the radio than they do reading the papers, and in consequence radio advertising has steadily increased while newspaper advertising has steadily declined. But each radio station must show some skill and not a little tact in putting on the right kind of sustaining program. This comes under the head of "public interest, convenience, and necessity," and the programs in question take the form of forums, debates, and talks on public issues for which the radio station receives no money and for which it often has to pay out money itself. Nor is this all. In order to forestall more government regulation, actual government competition, or—most horrible of all—a government radio monopoly such as exists everywhere in Europe, the National Association of Broadcasters has set up a rigid code of its own. By self-regulation, it tries to set itself such high standards that the government will not try to impose higher ones. Moreover, to assert their independence of sponsors, the big radio chains insist on retaining control over many of the so-called "educational" features, like "America's Town Meeting of the Air," which could easily be sold to a sponsor not only because of its wide appeal but because it comes at a desirable time of day.

To sum up, then, the radio industry must appeal to the following interests in connection with its news broadcasts —or, indeed, any other program:

1. The Federal government.
2. Present or potential sponsors.
3. The listening public.
4. The radio industry itself.

A controversial commentator frightens away sponsors and therefore makes little appeal to any of the networks or the larger stations. Entirely apart from the radio industry's fear of offending the Federal government, it is equally afraid of offending public opinion. Not all newspaper publishers have Hearst's crusading zeal; few of them actually subordinate business considerations to political considerations. But most newspaper publishers use their papers to wield political as well as economic power. The men who control the radio industry have just the same concern—no more, no less—with public opinion as the men who control any other public utility. This does not mean they are indifferent to the public. It means that they are sensitive about their own industry and they are also as eager as the advertising manager of any newspaper not to offend any section of the public.

The radio industry has worked out two methods of avoiding offense and promoting controversy. The Federal Communications Commission permits time to be sold for the discussion of political issues during political campaigns and leaves it to the radio industry to apportion the time fairly among all parties on the ballot. But the code of the National Association of Broadcasters goes farther. In order to prevent any one group with a lot of money from buying up too much time for the discussion of controversial issues, the code expressly forbids the sale of any time for any controversial issue except during political campaigns. It does, however, urge the individual stations to air controversial issues by staging debates on free time or else giving the different sides of any controversy an equal opportunity to

163

be heard. This avoids giving offense; it provides some excitement and diversity; it does not favor any special interest. The result is that such unsponsored, sustaining programs as "America's Town Meeting of the Air," "The People's Platform," and "The People's Forum" have large audiences. Here, if nowhere else, the listener gets honest and sharp, if somewhat confused, differences of opinion.

The news associations and the syndicates dominate the newspaper industry; four great networks dominate radio. Not only do these networks reach every corner of the country; they present much the best programs, they have the most powerful transmission stations, they almost always come through more clearly than small, local stations. The National Broadcasting Company controls two networks, the Columbia Broadcasting System and the Mutual Broadcasting System one each. As far as the coverage and interpretation of the news is concerned, these three great corporations, the men behind them, and the men who talk over them control just about everything most of us hear over the radio. This concentration of control, I repeat, is more or less inherent in the very nature of radio. It would be physically impossible to maintain more stations, and if most of those we have did not belong to chains they could not pay their way. The government supervises the industry, but the industry regulates itself, and real competition exists. Radio is not yet a monopoly on the order of the American Telephone and Telegraph Company.

What is the nature of the three big radio companies and

the men behind them? After the last war, Rockefeller and Morgan money provided most of the original financing for the National Broadcasting Company. Actually, the National Broadcasting Company is owned by the Radio Corporation of America which makes radio sets. NBC also ties in with General Electric and Westinghouse, each of which owns a station. David Sarnoff, chairman of the board of NBC and president of RCA, got his start working with Marconi. He is a radio man from way back and grew up with the industry. Most of the other directors of NBC, however, are better known for their industrial and banking connections. They have an educational expert in the person of ex-President James Rowland Angell of Yale, who belongs to the great tradition of academic conservatism— a worthy peer of A. Lawrence Lowell of Harvard and Nicholas Murray Butler of Columbia.

Although radio is a relatively young industry, NBC's two networks are run by relatively old men who received their training in other fields. The Columbia Broadcasting System, on the other hand, has younger men controlling it all along the line. It grew out of another young industry —motion pictures—and was controlled by Paramount-Publix until 1932, when the Harriman interests took over and challenged—not for the first time—the Morgan interests. William S. Paley, president of CBS, is a man of liberal views who has not yet turned forty. Herbert Bayard Swope, one of his fellow directors, is the brother of Gerard Swope of General Electric and as executive editor of the

New York *World* gave that newspaper its distinctive character during the 1920's. Other board members include representatives of Lehman Brothers and Brown Brothers. NBC, on the other hand, has on its board such old-timers as General Charles G. Dawes and General James G. Harbord. CBS has pioneered more than NBC, especially in news coverage. In H. V. Kaltenborn it developed the first modern news commentator, and its roundups of foreign news at the time of the Munich crisis set a pattern that has become standard.

The Mutual Broadcasting System is a producer's co-operative, owned and controlled by 154 stations throughout the country. The chief of these is the powerful WOR Station, owned by the Bamberger department store in Newark. Bamberger's is an affiliate of R. H. Macy and Company, and Macy's is largely controlled by the Straus family. The late Jesse Isidor Straus, former president of Macy's, served as ambassador to France and supported Roosevelt even before the Democratic Convention of 1932. Richard Weil, the president of Bamberger's, is also chairman of the board of WOR, key station in the Mutual network. His father was a doctor; his mother was the sister of Percy Straus, chairman of the board of R. H. Macy. At thirty-three, Richard Weil is one of the most phenomenally successful young men in America, and his interests extend beyond department stores and radio into the purely academic field. A student of Korzybski and the science of semantics, he belongs to the Robert Hutchins-Mortimer

166

Adler school of liberalism rather than the John Dewey-George Counts variety.

The full-time head man in the Mutual Broadcasting System is its president, Alfred Justin McCosker. A Democrat just turned sixty, Mr. McCosker has had a varied career, first as a reporter on Midwestern newspapers, then as editor of a movie trade journal, and from 1918 to 1924 as public relations counsel for the American Federation of Labor. He went to work for Bamberger's in 1922 and has served as president of Mutual since 1934.

The Mutual Broadcasting System with its 154 stations is the largest of the networks, but it is not controlled by any substantial concentration of big money. Moreover, in many localities, its stations have not got the prestige, the power, or the following of the NBC and CBS stations. In so far as the Mutual stations have any political tendency, they would tend to be New Dealish. Columbia is liberal, but not necessarily pro-Roosevelt. NBC is decidedly the most conservative of the three big radio companies.

Some localities have developed powerful independent stations that do not take programs from any of the networks. There are also a number of smaller chains. But it would require a whole book to list the interests behind these individual stations, few of which reach more than one section of the country. This is not to minimize the influence of the independent stations. Whereas all the stations connected with any of the networks belong to the National Association of Broadcasters and observe its code,

167

many of the independent stations do not belong to the NAB. Father Coughlin, for instance, went on paying for time to discuss controversial issues, and since his station did not belong to the NAB it even refused the opponents of Father Coughlin equal time to reply to his broadcasts. The independent stations also have countless local speakers who discuss everything under the sun from domestic science to international relations. Such is the prestige of radio that many an ignorant layman believes he has only to get his face within a foot of any live microphone and the whole country is listening to him. Actually, the small stations find the going difficult. Because few of them can afford to pay for their unsponsored programs, they run to news programs which cost little or nothing and which also find wide acceptance. According to Mr. Lazarsfeld's book, there are four times as many local news programs as there are national news programs, whereas only half of all the other programs heard on the air originate in a local studio. Since most listeners like to keep their radio tuned to one station, it would seem that the tendency is to listen to local news dispatches but for entertainment to rely on the chains.

11

THE MEN BEHIND THE MICROPHONES

☆ ☆ ☆ ☆ ☆

NEWS PROGRAMS fall into three main categories. First, there are the straight news broadcasts, read by an announcer or a "newscaster" and prepared by one of the three press associations or by Transradio News, an independent service designed only for radio stations. Second, there are the news analysts, or commentators as they are now called, some of whom specialize in forecasts, analysis, and news behind the news, but most of whom do little more than summarize the news bulletins, throwing in an occasional editorial comment. Although the radio commentator corresponds to the newspaper columnist he keeps his own opinions much more in the background. What he exploits is not a point of view but a voice, a manner, a distinctive way of speaking. Finally, to provide a clash of opinion, there is the forum, debate, or round-table type of program which has become increasingly popular and which specializes in opinion.

The National Broadcasting Company now commands the services of the two most popular news broadcasters in radio—Lowell Thomas and H. V. Kaltenborn. Thomas summarizes the news of the day five times a week; Kaltenborn, who talks less frequently, specializes in interpretation. Both men pioneered in their respective fields and built up the first big audiences for a type of news program that has become identified with their two names. What sort of human beings are they?

Lowell Thomas, at forty-eight, has a life of adventure behind him. He attended four colleges, working his way through each but never graduating from any, and shortly after he came of age he headed two expeditions to the subarctic. He liked to write, take pictures, and talk, and soon developed great skill as a lecturer. When the United States entered the World War, Thomas received a special assignment from President Wilson to cover its history and visited all the principal fronts with a staff of cameramen and assistants. He made his supreme scoop in Arabia where he joined General Allenby, met T. E. Lawrence, and brought out the first story of the dramatic desert campaign. He has delivered his Lawrence-Allenby lecture 4000 times to 4,000,000 people.

In 1930, Lowell Thomas began broadcasting over an NBC network. He had by this time made a speaking tour all over the world, accompanied the Prince of Wales on a trip through India, and brought to America the first comprehensive story concerning the effects of the war on Central Europe. Today, Lowell Thomas' voice is as familiar as President Roosevelt's. Not only does he talk on the radio, he recites a weekly commentary to accompany one of the newsreels. But the amount of work he does and the wide audience to which he must appeal have prevented him from expressing any opinion with which the great majority of the American people are not already in agreement. Indeed, ever since his early days, he has steered away from controversial subjects and has preferred to emphasize drama and personality in the news.

H. V. Kaltenborn carries the weight of the world on his shoulders. To him the news is not a spectacle to be dramatically reported but a succession of moral issues to be conscientiously expounded. In other words, while Lowell Thomas ministers to the American people's love of sensation, H. V. Kaltenborn ministers to their moral sense. Like Thomas, Kaltenborn had an adventurous youth. Born sixty-two years ago of Midwestern German stock, he ran away from home at twenty to volunteer in the Spanish-American War and came back a sergeant. He then went to work on a small-town newspaper, quit his job a year later to go to France for a year as a traveling salesman, and returned to the United States in 1902 when he went to work for the *Brooklyn Eagle*. Whereas Lowell Thomas attended four colleges before he came of age, Kaltenborn enrolled at Harvard as a special student while he was still working for the *Eagle* and was graduated in 1909 at the age of thirty-one with a degree *cum laude*, a Phi Beta Kappa Key, and two prizes for debating and public speaking.

This record attracted the attention of John Jacob Astor who hired Kaltenborn as traveling tutor for his son Vincent for a year. Kaltenborn then returned to the *Eagle*, remaining with the paper until 1930 and serving as drama editor, editorial writer, assistant manager, and associate editor. He also made annual trips to Europe, Latin America, and the Far East and began his enormously successful career as a lecturer. Kaltenborn made his debut on the radio back in 1921 when an address of his to the Brooklyn Chamber of Commerce was broadcast from Newark. In 1923 he began a weekly half-hour chat on the news over Station WEAF of the National Broadcasting Company.

In 1930, Kaltenborn left his job on the *Eagle* to become news editor for the Columbia Broadcasting System, where he remained for the next ten years. He interviewed celebrities all over the world, won a gold medal in 1936 for broadcasting from the front-line trenches in Spain, but it was not until 1938 that his running, spontaneous commentary on the Munich crisis made him the national figure that he is today. The urgency of this crisis called for a new technique and a deeper understanding of the news, and Kaltenborn's long experience made him the man of destiny at that particular juncture.

In the October, 1939, issue of *Current History* Kaltenborn defined the purpose of his broadcasts on the present war as follows: "Today, my one dominant purpose is to keep America out of the war. That is why I am doing my best to be neutral." Calling attention to the many nationalities represented in the United States he added, "to take sides would stir up hatred and conflict among our own people, and thus would make it more difficult to preserve peace." But with the Norwegian, Dutch, Belgian, French, and British campaigns, Kaltenborn's original views changed—whose have not?—and he became a more open partisan of the Allied cause. The fact that he is himself of German extraction and that his wife is a German baroness give him special insight into the German mentality and probably cause him to lean over backward to avoid any suspicions of pro-German sympathy. But in his present tendency to regard Hitler as the root of all evil, Kaltenborn has become indistinguishable from those Americans who can think of American problems only in terms of defending the British Empire.

The National Broadcasting Company acknowledged the superior news coverage of the Columbia Broadcasting System when it took over H. V. Kaltenborn in the spring of 1940. Ever since the Munich crisis, NBC had experimented with commentators of its own—John Gunther, H. R. Baukhage, T. R. Ybarra, Lowell Thomas—but it did not develop an equivalent of Kaltenborn; neither did its European representatives do as good a job rounding up the news of the foreign capitals as the representatives of Columbia. Meanwhile, CBS was developing a new commentator with still a different technique, and now Elmer Davis is carrying on where Kaltenborn left off.

NBC suffers from overorganization and an overdose of vested interests. Frederick Bate, for instance, who has represented NBC in Europe since 1932, has lived abroad since 1912. In 1919 he became associated with the Reparations Commission and remained with it until it was dissolved in 1930. Ten years in the society of bureaucrats do not stimulate one's news sense; yet it was no doubt this experience, crowned by two years with an American banking house in Paris, that commended Bate to NBC. But NBC has paid dearly for its conservatism and although it has uncovered some effective individual broadcasters —notably Max Jordan in Berlin and William Hillman in London—its coverage of world news lags behind that of CBS.

Nothing brings out this contrast more clearly than the personalities and backgrounds of Frederick Bate on the one hand and CBS's Edward R. Murrow on the other. Murrow, still on the sunny side of forty, is a graduate of Leland Stanford and headed the National Student Federation from 1930–32. This was supposed to get the United States into the League of Nations, but it later became a New Deal agency, and from 1932 to 1935 Murrow held the post of assistant director of the Institute of International Education which is financed by Rockefeller and Carnegie money. Murrow once wrote a book with James T. Shotwell called *Channels of International Co-operation* and thus qualifies as an authentic heir to the Woodrow Wilson tradition. His "line," in so far as he has one, therefore parallels that of the Roosevelt Administration, and though Frederick Bate of NBC no doubt shares most of Edward Murrow's convictions, he does not put them across so effectively.

Since 1937, when Murrow went over to London to replace Cesar Saerchinger as head of the CBS European staff, he has worked out a technique of his own in covering crises. The reporter who speaks from a foreign city should avoid news that American listeners have already heard through other channels; he must also operate under a censorship and talk from a script. The American reporters abroad therefore concentrate on local color with the result that there is scarcely a taxi driver west of Moscow whose views on the international situation are not known to every family in the United States. Murrow, however, has long since discarded that particular source of information, just as he also had to give up some time ago the interviews with European celebrities in which Saerchinger had specialized. For the past year and more, Murrow and his colleagues on the European staff of CBS have created an entirely new type of reporting which combines news, opinion, and local color. Whereas Paul Archinard, the NBC man in Paris, simply rehashed the government handouts, Eric Severeid of CBS went out and dug up his own stories, often at great personal risk. Few newspapermen showed as much initiative and courage in running down original stories.

Most American radio reporters abroad—like most of our foreign correspondents—detest Hitler. Nearly all of them also have become so Europeanized that they believe the United States should permanently associate itself with Europe and permanently throw its weight behind a balance of power that will prevent Germany from dominating the Continent. William S. Hillman, who used to represent Hearst in London and who is now European representative of *Collier's*, has less crusading spirit than many of his colleagues. He has preserved a relatively detached point of view and has not lost touch with the American mentality. During the first winter of the war, his talks for NBC gave the best analysis and the most accurate forecasts of any that came from the other side. But perhaps the fact that he was operating most of the time from England where speech was still relatively free made his job a little easier.

In Germany, of course, American radio reporters work under a close censorship, and the amazing thing is that they manage to get so many impressions through. Columbia's William Shirer, for instance, finds life under the Nazis such an ordeal that he has to step outside Germany to Switzerland once in a while for a breath of fresh air. Yet, curiously enough, Shirer of CBS and Max Jordan of NBC manage to tell more about Germany than we get in most of our newspapers. The very handicaps under which they operate plus the fact that their voices actually come from German territory give their broadcasts a dramatic quality of their own.

It hardly seems worth while to list and characterize all the European reporters of both NBC and CBS; the

176

careers of Max Jordan and William Shirer indicate clearly what kind of people report the news from Europe to the United States over the radio. Max Jordan was born in Italy forty-five years ago of Austro-German and French parents. He grew up in Italy, Germany, and Switzerland and made occasional trips to France. He took his Ph.D. in philosophy at Jena and hoped to become a professor of religious philosophy, but in 1920 he went to work for a newspaper syndicate in Berlin. Two years later he became Karl Von Wiegand's assistant and soon he was traveling all over the world on newspaper assignments. In 1931 he made his present connection with NBC.

William Shirer is as American as Jordan is European. Still under forty he came to Europe on a shoestring in 1925 and landed a job with the *Chicago Tribune*. He remained with that paper for seven years, covering all parts of Europe. He has even visited India where he became an admirer of Gandhi whom he calls "the greatest man of our times." In 1932 Shirer went to work for CBS in Vienna, married a Viennese wife, and has remained with the organization ever since. Thus, one of the men who reports on Hitler's Germany to American radio listeners is a Ph.D. in religious philosophy and the other considers Gandhi the greatest man alive.

Whereas NBC and CBS maintain a full-time staff in several European capitals, the Mutual Broadcasting System confines itself to commissioning occasional talks by newspaper correspondents. John Steele who talks for Mutual from London on alternate Sundays calls himself an American and is, in fact, a naturalized American citizen. Steele was born in Belfast in 1870, came to this country at the age of fifteen, worked on newspapers in New York, became a citizen at the age of twenty-three, but has lived in London since 1919 where he represented the *Chicago Tribune* until 1935. Since then he has retired from active newspaper work and his chief activity now is handling the affairs of the Mutual Broadcasting System in Europe.

Lack of funds has prevented the Mutual Broadcasting System from covering Europe as extensively as NBC and Columbia do. But freedom from stuffed-shirt control has enabled Mutual to score in other directions. It pioneered in rebroadcasting foreign news programs. These are picked up in the United States via short wave, recorded, and then sent out here via long wave. Mutual has also assembled an excellent staff of military and naval experts —Major Leonard Nason for land operations, Paul Schubert for naval operations, and Colonel Charles W. Kerwood for the war in the air.

Columbia's Major George Fielding Eliot stands out nevertheless as the most popular of the military experts. He writes a column several times a week for the *New York Herald Tribune* and contributes often to *Life*. He owes his eminence to several books he wrote before the war broke out. The first—and best—was *If War Comes*, on which he collaborated with Major Dupuy. Then came *The Ramparts We Watch*, which might have been written by a retired admiral because of its emphasis on the importance of sea power to America. Even before the war began, Major Eliot saw he had gone a little too far, and in *Bombs Bursting in Air*, a shorter book, he explained the importance of air power.

Major Eliot is a Midwest American who was living in Australia when the last war broke out and served with the Australian forces at Gallipoli. Although he holds a reserve commission in the United States Army, he has combined with his study of military strategy the practice of writing fiction for the pulp magazines. This enabled him to develop an easy style that has helped to cover up some of his errors, notably his prophecy in the early stages of the German-Polish war that "General Mud" would stop Hitler. But Major Eliot has two powerful recommendations—the gift of gab and a strong, attractive personality. He writes fast and speaks easily on his feet.

While Columbia has excelled the other networks in its coverage of foreign news, Mutual's outstanding achievement has been the development of Raymond Gram Swing as the leading American news commentator. It is quite in line with the whole Mutual setup that Swing is the most liberal commentator on any national network; that he should also be the first national commentator to join William Allen White's Committee to Defend America by Aiding the Allies does not detract from his liberalism; not at all. The chief indicator of American liberalism today is the intensity of one's hatred of Hitler, and Swing's long residence in Europe, his love of England, and his frequent contributions to *The Nation* leave no doubt about where he stands.

Raymond Gram Swing is the son of a Congregational minister, and he was born fifty-three years ago in upper New York State. He was then brought up in Oberlin, Ohio, where he attended Oberlin Academy and the Oberlin Conservatory of Music. A gifted piano student, he was never graduated from college but went into newspaper work and at the age of twenty-four became managing editor of the *Indianapolis Star*. In 1913 he went to Berlin as Central European correspondent for the *Chicago Daily News* and covered the war from Belgium to the Dardanelles. When America entered the fighting, Swing became an examiner for the War Labor Board; in 1919 he returned to Berlin for the *New York Herald*, remaining there until 1922. The next two years he directed the foreign service of the *Wall Street Journal* and from 1924 to 1934 he covered London for the *Philadelphia Public Ledger*. Returning again to the United States he did a weekly broadcast for the British Broadcasting Corporation on "Things American" and wrote dispatches from New York for the London *News-Chronicle*. Already, in 1935, he was warning the American people against a native Fascism, and his book *Forerunners of American Fascism* met the fate of many another excellent work which the public is not sufficiently educated to understand.

Meanwhile, Swing kept his hand in writing for *The*

Nation, and in 1937 he began commenting on the news for the Mutual Broadcasting System. He had the hard luck to be in Europe during the Munich crisis, but on his return he refused to follow the Kaltenborn pattern of ad-libbing his remarks and always insisted on talking from a prepared typescript. His prudence stood him in good stead. He did not go on the air too frequently, and when he did he had something to say and said it effectively. Compare his little book *How War Came,* made up of his prepared broadcasts from early 1939 until the war broke out, with *Kaltenborn Covers the Crisis,* an ad-libbed story of the events of the fall of 1938, and you will see what progress has occurred in this one field.

Elmer Davis, the third most popular radio commentator and the most recent arrival in the field, differs from the other two in the possession of a typically American sense of humor. Neither Kaltenborn nor Swing could possibly have written *Friends of Mr. Sweeney,* an hilarious best seller of the 1920's, satirizing the kept magazine business and celebrating its author's departure from the regular staff of *The New York Times.* Elmer Davis has expressed sympathy for Socialism, but today he would barely qualify as a liberal, since he does not have such a low moral boiling point as either Kaltenborn or Swing.

Just turned fifty, Elmer Davis is Indiana born and bred, and even three years in Oxford as a Rhodes scholar failed to dent his Hoosier accent. They did, however, dispose him to admire the British, a tendency that ten years on

The New York Times staff did not diminish. Between 1914 and 1924, the *Times* all but achieved Dominion status, and Davis wrote a history of the paper. From 1924 until the war crisis of 1939 he devoted most of his time to free-lance writing, specializing in essays, light fiction, book reviews, and feature articles. He now holds a position on the staff of *The Saturday Review of Literature* as well as his job with Columbia. His leading article in the April, 1940, issue of *Harper's* defined his stand on the war. He expressed the hope that the United States could keep out, argued against sending troops abroad, but warned against the assumption that the war could not come over here. He also cited the example of England to show that a democracy at war did not necessarily sacrifice, even for the duration, all the liberties for which it was fighting. Some pacifists complained that he had become war-minded, but he certainly did not go so far as the extreme interventionists, though of course he never had any use for isolation.

The Munich crisis of 1938 made Kaltenborn's reputation. The outbreak of war in 1939 put Swing and Davis on the map. Each of these three men, furthermore, expresses a point of view that does no violence to the interests that control the network over which he speaks. They have all established themselves as strong enough personalities in their own right to attract sponsors who, knowing what they stand for, make no attempt to influence their views. But several other commentators who also discuss world affairs over national hookups also deserve some mention.

Wythe Williams has demonstrated what a newspaper-man with a good European background, fresh contacts, and the courage to guess in public can do over the air. One year short of sixty, Williams lived in Europe from 1910 to 1937. He has worked for *The New York Times* and Hearst, for *The Saturday Evening Post* and *Collier's*. He has headed news bureaus in Berlin, London, Paris, and Geneva. He is a former president of the International Association of Journalists accredited to the League of Nations and of the Anglo-American Press Club of Paris. He covered the whole of the last war on the Western Front and visited the United States shortly afterward on a propaganda tour for the devastated regions of France.

Williams knows Europe and European news as well as any American talking on the air. He also hears a great many stories—not all of them, by any means, true—from an enormous variety of acquaintances. His knowledge and his common sense tell him what to discount, whereupon he takes a long breath and jumps off the deep end into the deep sea of prophecy. Of course, he sometimes doesn't come up at all; sometimes he comes part way up or appears in an unexpected spot; more often, though, his prophecies turn out all right. What he does, however, is not to analyze or interpret the news; he frankly engages in a one-man guessing game and takes the American people into his confidence. Williams is not "showing up" the commentators or newscasters. Many of them would

183

come to the same conclusions. He is simply doing a different job. He does not deal entirely with verified news, but even the verified dispatches are not one hundred per cent accurate, and therefore his record compares favorably even with those of his more cautious colleagues.

In Gabriel Heatter the Mutual Broadcasting System has one of the most popular news broadcasters and radio personalities. Heatter, however, can hardly be classified as a commentator. His function is to heighten still further by vocal inflection and phrasing news that is already exciting enough. Heatter achieved nation-wide fame in a single hour when he talked for fifty-two minutes without stopping and without a script on April 6, 1936, the night of the Bruno Richard Hauptmann execution. Heatter got his start in radio when Donald Flamm, president of Station WMCA in New York, read a reply Heatter had written to an article by Norman Thomas in *The Nation* on the subject of Socialism. Heatter read his piece over the air and was signed up as a commentator forthwith. Since then, he has become more and more a personality, especially in his popular "We, the People" program, where he has established himself as a showman of genius. Like Lowell Thomas, he has preferred to become a promoter, rather than a molder of public opinion. Which has vastly increased his audience while restricting his influence.

If Gabriel Heatter is Mutual's equivalent of Lowell Thomas, Edwin C. Hill does the same job for Columbia. Like Heatter and Thomas, Hill specializes in dramatizing the news—and himself. Like them he has a distinctive voice and delivery. Like them he has a newspaper background—he still writes a column for Hearst—but he steers aways from controversial issues. Although most of the highly paid radio commentators have a conservative point of view, they support the administration on the war issue if only because alarmist prowar talk sounds more exciting than the conciliatory voice of peace. Passing mention should also be made of Paul Sullivan of Columbia and Arthur Hale of Mutual. These two men should be classified as newscasters because they simply read, in rather impressive baritone voices, summaries of the news.

During the last year, the three big radio chains have all set up Washington bureaus. Hilmar Robert Baukhage has had a long career as a newspaperman in Europe and Washington. In 1932 he covered the White House for David Lawrence's *United States News* and when the present war began he reported on it from Europe for NBC. Soon, however, he was shifted to Washington and now heads the NBC bureau there. Fifty-one years old, the descendant of a Prussian supreme court judge who later became an officer in the Union Army and then pioneered in the Northwest, Baukhage is kindly, conservative, and decidedly a square peg in a square hole.

Fulton Lewis, Jr., who speaks from Washington for the Mutual Broadcasting System, was born in the national capital thirty-six years ago and went to work at twenty as a cub reporter on the *Washington Herald*. Three years later he became managing editor and started his radio career reading news flashes from a small local station. He then spent nine years covering Washington for the International News Service and in 1937 started a local news program over Station WOL, Mutual's Washington affiliate. He is one of the few commentators with a national audience who occasionally criticizes Administration foreign policy.

In 1939 the Radio Correspondents Association in Washington elected Lewis their president. In 1940, Albert Warner, head of Columbia's Washington bureau succeeded him. Warner had just quit one of the most important newspaper jobs in Washington—he was head of the *New York Herald Tribune's* bureau there—to enter this new field. Still under forty, he worked on newspapers from 1924 to 1939. He covered the World Economic Conference at London in 1933 and since 1931 has worked closely with the State Department. He therefore has a seasoned, mildly conservative, and decidedly world-minded slant on Washington news.

This survey shows that radio news falls into the following categories:

1. News broadcasts prepared by the press associations or by Transradio News. This is exactly the same news that you get in your paper, boiled down and then respiced with adjectives for radio presentation.

2. News commentators. These correspond to the news-

186

paper columnists, but most of them summarize the news more than they interpret it.

3. Roundups of foreign and domestic news. These are a unique radio feature and give a firsthand, informal, personal impression of what is happening at Washington and in the various news centers abroad. They also include reports from military and naval experts.

The news programs now on the air correspond more or less to the policies of the various chains over which they are heard. The Columbia Broadcasting System does the best all-round job of news coverage; it is more enterprising and youthful than NBC, more comprehensive and authoritative than Mutual. But Mutual has the best all-round military coverage—with the possible exception of Major George Fielding Eliot of Columbia—and the most original commentator in Raymond Gram Swing. Mutual and Columbia have more liberal managements than NBC; their commentators therefore sound a trifle more friendly to Roosevelt. All the networks, however, have accepted Roosevelt's foreign policy, and since Boake Carter's voice ceased upon the midnight air, no strong dissenter has spoken regularly on a national network. Only if Carter comes back, stays back, and hits back can the New Deal deny that it has deliberately squelched one of its most effective critics on the air.

For unorthdox or minority opinion, the listener must turn to individual talks and to the radio discussion groups. Theodore Grannik's "People's Forum," broadcast every

Sunday night from Washington, provides the most fireworks, but it concentrates on political issues and most of its speakers are Congressmen, Senators, and public officials. "America's Town Meeting of the Air," conducted by George V. Denny, Jr., has perhaps the greatest prestige, although the "University of Chicago Round Table" and CBS's "People's Platform," conducted by Professor Lyman Bryson, claim larger audiences. All these, however, are genuine debates in which the participants talk as they please and in which all points of view are heard.

The chief asset of radio is that it is a young and growing industry: radio revenue from advertising rose from $20,-000,000 in 1928 to $170,000,000 in 1939. Except in 1933, each year showed an increase over the year before. Meanwhile, during the same decade, the advertising revenue of magazines and newspapers steadily declined—in the case of newspapers more than one third, in the case of magazines more than one quarter. Not until radio stops growing is it likely to abandon the progressive policies it has followed up to now.

THE COMMENTATORS

☆ ☆ ☆ ☆ ☆

RADIO STATIONS do not customarily broadcast the sun, moon, and tide schedules issued by the United States Coast and Geodetic Survey. In reproducing the style of the radio commentators, I am therefore going to take the corresponding item in the field of radio—the weather report—and show how different people would comment on a forecast of continued heat, followed by thunderstorms in the late afternoon.

And now—to coin a phrase—Lowell Thomas:

The blinding sands of Asia Minor. The copper surface of the Red Sea. The sun, a hot ball of fire, slowly lifts itself above the eastern horizon. Another day has begun. It is a windless, cloudless day, a day of burning heat such as only the deserts of Arabia can know. Only the deserts of Arabia and perhaps the mountains of central Tibet, the African veldt, the mining country of Central Australia, the green hell of the Mato Grosso in unexplored Brazil, and our Black Hills of the Dakotas. But as the day draws to a close, thunderheads appear in the northwest. Light-

189

ning flashes. Thunder booms. Great drops of rain fall on the parched earth. The season of floods has begun and the shepherd folk hurry to the hills. And here, too, in this great land of ours, the weather has its way with us. Here, too, the heat wave makes our sidewalks sizzle like those delicious Southern Mammy pancakes, the kind that Mother —yes and Grandma—used to make. I can taste them now. Yum. Yum.

H. V. Kaltenborn speaking:

The latest weather report, forecasting continued heat followed by thundershowers in the late afternoon, may well upset the balance of power in Europe. If the skies remain clear throughout the day, German airplanes will not be able to attack Britain. However, if clouds gather at night, British airplanes, taking advantage of the obscurity will be able to bomb Germany. But how about Russyah? That is another story. If the skies remain clear throughout the day, it would be quite in keeping with the character of shrewd, pipe-smoking Joseph Stalin to surprise the mercurial, vegetable-eating Adolf Hitler with a daytime raid because that is the time when the German dictator would least expect it. But what would the bald and wily Benito Mussolini be doing all this while? Ah, if we knew the answer to that question we might be able to guess how crabbed old Marshal Pétain and oily Pierre Laval with his white necktie would respond. Meanwhile continued droughts are likely to ruin the olive crop in Spain, and even thundershowers can yield little benefit because the eroded earth of the parched Iberian peninsula retains no moisture. Thus, the banks of the Ebro and the Tagus, where I have walked many a time, will be likely to overflow, spreading destitution in their wake. And who will profit from all this misery? Ah, if we could answer that question, then we might be able to penetrate the secret places of the heart of Adolf Hitler. And if we could find what plans Germany's little corporal has for Europe, Asia, Africa, America, the world—yes and the sun, moon, and stars —then we might be able to plan our own defenses and know whether we shall have to repel an attack of Germans or an attack of Martians. As it is, I haven't the slightest idea. Have you? Good night.

At this point the Columbia Broadcasting System presents a roundup of the foreign capitals, followed by an analysis of the military situation, by Columbia's military expert, Major George Fielding Eliot:

ANNOUNCER: *Hello, London; Hello, London; Hello, London.*

Pause

ANNOUNCER: *CBS New York calling London. Come in, London.*

This is Ed Murrow speaking from London, England. I have just returned from spending the week end in a little fishing village on the coast of Cornwall. I cannot tell you its name, but no matter. I sought out this fishing village

191

because the weather bureau had forecast a clear, hot day with scattered thundershowers in the afternoon, and I hoped I might get a real view of a German bombardment. Unfortunately it rained all day and a heavy fog set in at night. The Germans did not attack, and I could not have seen anything if they had. I now return you to the Columbia Broadcasting System in New York.

ANNOUNCER: Thank you, London. We now take you to Berlin. Hello, Berlin. CBS New York calling Berlin. Come in, Berlin.

Berlin speaking. I have just returned from spending the week end in a little fishing village on the coast of Baltic. I cannot tell you its name, but no matter. I sought out this fishing village because the weather bureau had forecast a clear, hot day with scattered thundershowers in the late afternoon, and I hoped I might get a real view of a British bombardment. Unfortunately it rained all day and a heavy fog set in at night. The British did not attack, and I could not have seen anything if they had. I now return you to the Columbia Broadcasting System in New York.

ANNOUNCER: Here in the studio we have Columbia's military expert, Major George Fielding Eliot, who will interpret the news you have just heard from Europe and other late dispatches. Major Eliot.

MAJOR ELIOT: Good evening. Interpreting these two reports we have just heard from London and Berlin, I should analyze them as follows from the military standpoint. The reporter in London said he could not see any

German raiders over British soil, but he said nothing about whether he could see British raiders over German soil. Of course, we have the testimony of the reporter in Berlin that he saw no British raiders over German soil, but you will note that he made no mention of German raiders over British soil. Each reporter therefore saw no enemy raiders, but neither reporter made any mention of what was happening in the other country. Most significantly, they confined their comments to what they could see in the countries from which they were speaking, and of course the fog prevented them from seeing anything anyway. The question therefore arises: were both of them speaking freely, was neither of them speaking freely, or was one of them speaking freely and the other being censored? And if one of them was speaking freely and the other was being censored, which one was speaking freely and which one was being censored? It is problems like these which make the task of the military expert the engrossing one that it is.

Meanwhile a dispatch has just arrived from London stating that clear weather throughout the British Isles enabled the Germans to undertake a series of technical reconnaissance flights which resulted in the elimination of the residential sections of several large British cities and all the inhabitants. Meanwhile, clear weather over Germany permitted the British to undertake air reprisals for the German technical reconnaissance flights. It is said that these reprisal flights attained their objectives.

Now, interpreting this latest news flash in the light of

the reports we have just received direct from Europe, it would appear that the war has reached a technical stalemate. Both sides appear to be executing important military maneuvers with a reasonable degree of success and the principal objectives in enemy territory seem to be attained. But neither side appears able to shift from the defensive to the offensive type of warfare. If this state of affairs continues for a protracted period, it will of course mean the complete liquidation of the entire civilian population. In short, the strategy and tactics of total war present a new perspective and one that the future military historian will study with pleasure and profit—always assuming there are any military historians left to derive pleasure and profit from studying the experiments now under way in that military laboratory which is modern Europe. Good night.

We take pleasure in presenting at this time Mutual's distinguished news analyst, Mr. Raymond Gram Swing:

The weather forecast of continued heat followed by thundershowers in the late afternoon must be accepted with the utmost reserve. On the one hand, weather forecasters have proved themselves to be on occasion less than infallible. On the other hand, unless some organized effort is made to forecast the weather, we shall not, as the vernacular has it, know enough to come in when it rains. But when I read this particular report in the context of the particular time at which it arrived, my eyes just about popped out of my head. Continued heat, followed by thunderstorms? What could this signify? On the one hand, it might mean an intensification of the German offensive. On the other hand, it might mean a relaxation of that offensive. Or again, it might have some devious bearing on the British war plans. In any event, there is no occasion whatever for sudden panic. At a time like this, Americans must keep absolutely calm. We must think things through, coldly, logically, not letting our emotions or sympathies sway our judgment, not being carried away by false sentiment, on the one hand, or yet lulled into a sense of false security, on the other. After all, this weather report stating that the present heat wave is going to be followed by thunderstorms does not mean the world is coming to an end. And yet I wonder. Without ministering in any way to the present wave of hysteria that has seized so many of our fellow citizens, I should be inclined to believe that such a sudden change in weather does mean that the world is coming to an end—not at once, of course. Indeed, I should look to see the world hold together at least until I have completed this analysis of the news. But after that —Good night.

And now—Elmer Davis, with the news:

While Italian sailors were landing at the Greek port of Patras at the outlet of the Corinth Canal, clear skies were reported over large sections of Central Europe. But as the afternoon wore on and the British fortifications at

Gibraltar were reduced to powder by a high-explosive bomb, thundershowers fell on the western Mediterranean. Meanwhile Stalin in the Kremlin and Chiang Kai-shek in his capital at Chungking planned to co-ordinate their armies in a counterattack against the Japanese troops along the Amur River. President Roosevelt, observing these developments from the White House lawn where a sudden cloudburst cut short the British ambassador's daily visit, contemplated the steps that the United States might take to meet the gathering crisis in the Balkans, the Mediterranean, and Central Asia. An expanded navy would be able to put the Italians in their place, a draft army of ten million men could readily bring order to Central Europe, and an enlarged air force—say half a million planes—could rout both the Chinese and the Japanese and make this country the master of Asia. Consultations with the British ambassador will be resumed tomorrow afternoon, weather permitting.

We conclude with a typical radio forum:

ANNOUNCER: This afternoon, the "University of Chicago Round Table" presents a spontaneous, unrehearsed debate on the subject, "Does the United States Weather Bureau further the cause of world peace?" The discussion will be led by Professor John Robinson, head of the Department of Human Relations in the University of Chicago. And may I remind you that this is the Round Table discussion of the University of Chicago to which you are listening? The second speaker on this "University of Chicago Round Table" discussion is the celebrated Professor James Smith, head of the Department of Meteorology in the University of Chicago. You see, we try to make these "University of Chicago Round Table" discussions just as comprehensive as possible. And finally, we have the eminent British lecturer, George Brown, who will spend the coming year as an exchange professor in the University of Chicago. And now, Professor Robinson:

ROBINSON: What we are discussing, gentlemen, is whether the United States Weather Bureau promotes the cause of world peace, and before asking you your views on the subject I want to make it quite clear that the program allows the utmost freedom of discussion and that we can all feel free to talk exactly as we please. Moreover, for my own part, and speaking as a person who knows nothing whatever about either peace or the United States Weather Bureau, I want to go on record as saying that I am completely in favor of peace and utterly opposed to the United States Weather Bureau. I know that it forecasts continued hot weather followed by thunderstorms, but what of it? Hoover said that prosperity was just around the corner. As I said at the time, what we need in the White House is a man of vision and courage, not a small-minded millionaire engineer who made his fortune working for British mining companies in the Malay States. Why, when I stop to think—

BROWN: Excuse me, Robinson, but I can't allow that aspersion at the British mining companies to pass unchallenged. It so happens that I'm an old China hand myself. I served as vice-consul at Gib for ten years before the FO shifted me to the ICS and then—

SMITH: I'm an old ICS man too—took a course at the International Correspondence School myself before I got my present post at Chicago.

BROWN: But, my dear Chumley, the ICS isn't this correspondence school you talk about, it's the Indian Civil Service. And I don't suppose that you in America have anything that resembles it in any way.

SMITH: See here, Robinson, I mean Brown, my name is Smith, and we have got something very much like the ICS in our own Weather Bureau.

ROBINSON: Now wait a minute, Smith, you're getting off the subject. Brown here was discussing the Indian Civil Service and here you go talking about the Weather Bureau. It's all very well to have free discussion, but we simply must stick to the subject, which brings me back to Hoover's relationship toward those British mining companies. Now, as the leader of this discussion, I can't see that our friend Brown has made any kind of case at all, and I'm going to ask him a simple question. Wait a minute, Brown, I haven't asked it yet. Now I have in my pocket a three-column letter I wrote to The New York Times. At least it would have been a three-column letter if the Times had had the space to print it. But they didn't, so I'm going to

198

read it here and in that way set the stage for the question that I am going to ask our good friend Brown.

SMITH: But I thought this was a discussion about the weather and that you, Robinson, were just going to lead the discussion and that Brown and I were going to argue it out.

ROBINSON: See here, Smith, enough is enough. I'll have only just enough time to read my letter as it is, so no more interruptions—please. After I have read my letter explaining why President Hoover should have been impeached, then perhaps we'll have a few minutes left for more discussion, but I doubt it. What we've had has been most stimulating and I'm sure that those of you who have been listening to this broadcast from the "University of Chicago Round Table" have a new understanding of the burning issues that we have covered.

12

AND HOW TO UNDERSTAND IT

☆ ☆ ☆ ☆ ☆

THE MAIN FUNCTION of this book up to now has been to analyze the raw materials of the news. Only in the second chapter did I give any indication of how to interpret this material. And there I merely urged that you try to arrive at some point of view or try to make up your mind in advance what you are looking for in the news—and what you are not looking for. Perhaps our review of the news sources has suggested some new approaches or stirred up some old prejudices. In any case, the time has come to suggest definite ways and means.

I shall conclude with twelve commandments, designed to help you understand the news. First, however, let me give some specific tips and general recommendations. For instance, newspapers frequently print the complete text of an important statement as well as a news story about the statement. Which should you read? Nine times out of ten, the news story tells you all you want to know. Do not bother with the complete text unless you have some strong personal interest in the speaker or the subject. You may also have been puzzled by dispatches from Washington and from the capitals abroad quoting "authoritative sources," "a spokesman for the Ministry of Foreign Affairs," "an unimpeachable authority," but mentioning no one by name. These stories deserve much more credence than gossip columns or radio prophets. Almost always they come from someone in authority. If they express an opinion, they mean that this is what some high official, possibly the head of the state, really believes but does not dare to say. If, on the other hand, such stories as these contain statements of fact, they deserve just as much credence as if the source were actually named. This does not mean they are true; all it means is that they have as much authority as anything else you read from people in high station in that part of the world.

This brings up the question of propaganda and censorship, which are really two sides of the same coin. What is propaganda? During the first months of the Second World War, a small minority of Americans who favored an immediate declaration of war against Germany complained that "the propaganda against propaganda" had paralyzed the nation. Therefore, they launched what can only be called a campaign of propaganda against the propaganda against propaganda. What had happened was this. During the First World War, the American people heard a great deal from England about the wickedness of the Germans and the virtue of the Allies. Perhaps the American people were a bit naïve at the time; anyway, they believed most of what they heard, and some of it later turned out to be false. But what really burned up the American people was not that the British had occasionally lied to us. What really burned us up was that the war did not yield the promised benefits. We blamed the British much more for not paying their war debt than we did for an occasional propaganda story which later turned out to be exaggerated or untrue.

Twenty years later, the deceptions of the last war assume an exaggerated importance in our minds. The fact of the matter is that it wasn't either the half-truths or the half-lies that persuaded us. We believed British war propaganda in 1917 because we wanted to believe it; we were just looking for an excuse to act as we did. The so-called propaganda simply provided the moral justification for going to war in 1917. And what burned up the American interventionists during the early months of the Second World War was not the propaganda against propaganda. It was their own failure to find a propaganda appeal that would work the way the British propaganda worked in 1917. And they failed because the American people did not want to believe that kind of propaganda at that time.

In other words, propaganda must be defined as any ideas that lead to action. There is no such thing as true propaganda or false propaganda. There is only propaganda that works and propaganda that does not work. Lord Bryce's faked reports of Belgian atrocities whipped up the war spirit in the United States. Sir Nevile Henderson's truthful *Failure of a Mission* left Americans unmoved. Yet Hitler, who learned his propaganda technique from the British and who says "the bigger the lie, the bigger the propaganda," has antagonized a hundred times as many Americans as he has attracted. Propaganda is nothing but means toward an end; only if you believe that you cannot achieve noble ends by base means will you refuse to use the lie as a form of propaganda.

In referring to Hitler's failure to win friends and influence people in the United States I have judged his propaganda in terms of its immediate results. But propaganda as Hitler uses it can cut two ways. On the one hand, it can, of course, achieve direct results, and his methods have yielded great success in Austria and the Sudeten region, not to mention Germany itself, where many people had some reason to support his program. But Hitler can use propaganda to divide a nation as well as to unite it. In France, for example, he played upon the existing differences in public opinion to create still further confusion. His aim here was not to convert the French to his point of view but to paralyze them. Yet Hitler could never have defeated France by means of propaganda alone. He started off with overwhelming military superiority and then proceeded to spread his propaganda on soil that was just as ready to receive it as the soil of the United States was ready to receive British propaganda in 1917. The difference is that in 1917 the United States wanted to receive war propaganda whereas in 1940 France wanted to receive defeatist propaganda.

To what extent does propaganda figure in our news? The special pleaders you discount in advance. They set out frankly to exhort and convert, and I have already indicated what the different special pleaders stand for. But this is not the sort of propaganda you need to worry about; it is out in the open. The propaganda to worry about is the kind that sneaks up on you in a news story, when you least expect it and when you are more or less inclined to believe what you are reading. Remember in this connection that successful propaganda must respect existing prejudices, even capitalize on them. The German Library of Information does not mention Hitler's anti-Semitism in its monthly news bulletin prepared for American consumption. Americans do not approve of anti-Semitism. Therefore, the German Library of Information dwells on the Nazi Strength Through Joy movement, the youth movement, the labor camps—all of which suggest similar American enterprises.

So, in sizing up propaganda in the news, watch for it in the unexpected places, and every time you feel your opinions shifting or your emotions being swayed, ask yourself what lies behind the words. I am not suggesting you discount these impulses. Perhaps you should obey them. But it will do no harm to understand them.

Here is another tip. Discount newspaper headlines. There is nothing subversive about them. They are designed to sell papers and to express simple ideas in short words. They cannot, therefore, fully describe the story that follows. Also, remember that the stories themselves are often cut, not so much for "policy" or "propaganda" purposes as because they run too long. For that reason seek out at least once a day a newspaper that prints the fullest possible dispatches. And don't worry too much about the writers you disagree with; they are not putting over anything on you. Don't be too concerned, either, about "the interests." The chief interest of most newspaper publishers is to sell papers.

What kind of propaganda do specific newspapers, correspondents, and broadcasters promote? Outside New York City, where the *Daily News*, the *New York Post*, and *PM* support Roosevelt, almost the entire press of the nation is anti-New Deal. Many of the Washington correspondents, however, write pro-New Deal dispatches in anti-New Deal papers. And in the matter of foreign policy, many conservative papers that attack the New Deal support the Roosevelt line abroad. The Hearst and Scripps-Howard chains, however, have become pretty consistently antiadministration. It is the other way around on the radio. There, not a single voice on a national network criticizes Roosevelt's foreign policy. Fulton Lewis, Jr., who talks from Washington for Mutual takes a somewhat critical attitude, and Kaltenborn sounds distinctly more conservative than the New Deal on domestic issues.

Censorship, the reverse side of the propaganda medal, functions much more vigorously abroad than in the United States. Here, it is only in the field of radio that there is anything like consistent censorship, and what there is of it is pretty mild. By and large, the American radio industry gives a greater variety of opinion than the newspapers and a much more even apportionment of time. On the other hand, radio does tend to pull its punches, and in the matter of foreign policy all regular radio news broadcasts gently, firmly, and consistently support Roosevelt to the exclusion of any other point of view. When Boake Carter criticized New Deal foreign policy over a nation-wide network he suffered the same fate that befell Ludwell Denny when he criticized New Deal foreign policy in a syndicated column. It remains to be seen—and heard—whether Carter's projected return to the air materializes and continues.

But where censorship really affects the news we get is abroad. Even before the Second World War began, most foreign nations had set up some kind of censorship. Indeed, the two nations with the tightest censorships—Japan and the Soviet Union—are technically at peace, as of late September. We sometimes assume that the function of a government censorship is to prevent foreign newspapermen from getting facts that they already know out of the country. This is true to a limited extent. But another purpose of censorship is to conceal military movements; that is why place names are so often deleted from war news. But when it is a matter of releasing certain facts of general interest to the outside world, the newspaper generally gets the better of the censorship in the long run.

Thus, Mussolini has never been able to keep his occasional ailments secret. Even Stalin could not suppress the news of the famine of 1932 for more than a few months. After all, the outside world cannot remain forever ignorant about the starvation of several million people. That is why few reputable correspondents or newspapers ever confirmed the perennial underground rumors of imminent German collapse. If conditions inside Germany had really been as bad as some of the enemies of the regime wanted to believe, the news could not have been kept secret indefinitely.

The collapse of France shows that it is not censorship but bad information that causes the greatest confusion. For twenty years, military experts had assured the world that the French had the finest army in Europe. The German air force and mechanized troops were fine, too, but the French had trained longer and they had built their Maginot Line. The German attack took the world by surprise not because the French censorship had prevented correspondents in France from writing the truth as they saw it. The German attack took the world by surprise because almost nobody in France or abroad knew how inadequate the French army was as compared with the German. The decadence of the French people, the "Fifth Column," the "strategy of terror," the Fascist sympathies of some of the "200 families" played a part, but the central truth was that the French armed forces suffered a crushing defeat which took the Germans themselves by surprise. Literally nobody knew the facts about the inadequate French preparations.

Any more big surprises that the war may bring are likely to arise in the same fashion. The British, on the whole, have been frank with their own people and with the outer world. Their spokesmen have said it would be a long war and they never talk as if victory would come of its own accord. The Germans are much more frank with the outer world than they are at home. It is in the occupied territories that their censorship really cracks down.

If you want to find out what is happening in any country under a censorship, you should pick out at least one correspondent there and read everything he writes. Keep this up for a few weeks and you will begin to read between the lines; you will be able to compare one day's dispatch with another's. Herbert Matthews of *The New York Times* and John Whitaker of the *Chicago Daily News* do a good job on Italy. Hugh Byas of *The New York Times* is the best man in Tokyo. Moscow is impossible. Even the press associations do not get out a daily story.

Everything that has been said about press censorship goes double for radio. All governments carefully scrutinize all scripts, but the radio dispenses general impressions rather than facts. The tone of the speaker's voice, the kind of material he presents, the contrast between one city and another, especially in one of the roundups of foreign capitals—these factors can all be made to add up to a definite impression that no censorship can block. And, as a matter of fact, only a government on the point of collapse will try to muzzle all the facts.

From the point of view of the layman, the big problem in connection with war news is not censorship, but a host of technical problems having to do with geography, military strategy, and technical phrasing. If you are seriously interested in war news, read the official communiqués issued by the high commands of the warring powers. They are written in technical language but contain a minimum of falsehood. In fact, they usually tell the truth and nothing but the truth. Where they fall down is in not giving the whole truth—until long after it has happened.

But unless you are a glutton for punishment, the official communiqués make dull reading and you will probably find yourself turning instead to the military experts and to reporters writing from the scene of action. To date, the military experts have not covered themselves with glory. If truth is the first casualty in time of war, the military expert is the second, especially when he prophesies or when he plays the part of Monday-morning quarterback. Military experts should write only about engagements that have actually occurred and should confine themselves to explaining those engagements in nontechnical language. Hanson W. Baldwin of *The New York Times* is one of the few men in this field who has had the good sense to stick to this one task. The rest have all gone off the deep end at one time or another. Yet, in spite of their shortcomings, the military experts give a clearer picture of the whole development of a war than the correspondents in the field. The correspondents bring the battlefield to your breakfast table, but they are so close to what is happening that their general conclusions—if any—are worse than useless. As for the radio, I have already recommended Major George Fielding Eliot and the experts of the Mutual system. Like Hanson Baldwin, they confine themselves to analyzing what has happened instead of crystal gazing into the plans of the general staffs.

Surveys of newspaper-reading habits show that comparatively few people read the editorial page. In many papers it is hard to find, and in many more it makes dull reading. Hearst tried to attract attention to his editorial features by setting them in large, black type on the back pages of his papers, but his readers paid little attention to them, and now most of his papers put their last page to more profitable use by selling it to advertisers. Yet anyone who aspires to some understanding of the news should make a point of looking at the editorial page every day. There the owners of the paper state their real policies frankly. Read what they have to say and you will at least know how much to discount the less obvious editorializing in other sections of the paper.

Also, if you want expert interpretation of world news, editorial writers frequently will give you a fresh slant. Of course, they vary tremendously from paper to paper, but there are a few who have national reputations. William Allen White of the *Emporia Gazette* stands out particularly; so does Herbert Agar of the Louisville *Courier-Journal*. The *Boston Globe* has a remarkable staff who compose the famous "Uncle Dudley" editorial; the *Daily News* of New York has also developed under Captain Patterson a distinctive, informal style and wields real influence. And do not neglect the "Letters to the Editor" section. Some newspapers use this feature as a means of publicizing ideas for which they do not want to assume direct responsibility. Almost always you will find here, too, some authentic "*Vox Populi*" who shows up the professional experts in the adjoining columns.

Most newspapers have one important feature that you will not find on the radio—a financial section. Lincoln Steffens used to accuse the papers of deliberately burying the most important news in their financial pages because most readers did not turn to them and could not understand them if they did. This still holds true. Financial writers simply cannot afford to engage in wishful thinking. They have got to show what the news means in terms of dollars and cents, in stock-market prices, in commodity prices, in foreign-exchange rates, and the rest. There isn't any short cut to understanding the financial page. But more than any other section of the paper, it must be approached with a definite point of view. You have got to know what you want to find, what sort of thing you want to read. The best formula is to watch in the regular news stories for references to financial topics and then look for items about those topics in the financial section. Also, if you have some specialty, whether it is Russia, petroleum reserves, or the gold standard, you will almost always find it discussed somewhere in the financial section. But if you start browsing around the financial section you will be lost —unless you get bored first.

These are counsels of perfection, and what makes them almost impossible to follow is the raw material on which we all work. For even the biggest-shot correspondent or commentator does not possess complete information; indeed, he is seldom at liberty to tell in full the incomplete story he does know. As for the omnipotent statesman, he may have more information, but he must respect public opinion which, in turn, is manipulated by the newspapers and the radio. In short, everybody lives in awe of everybody else. The publisher and the advertiser cower before the writer's brains and the statesman's office. The writer cringes before the money of his employer and the statesman's superior knowledge and power. And all the while, the man in the street regards with even greater awe all these individuals who, ultimately, depend for their very existence on him. It isn't, perhaps, a vicious circle, but it is certainly a confused and confusing one.

I have touched this circle at several points and perhaps flew off on a tangent each time. Let me therefore review and summarize in the form of twelve commandments the main principles to keep in mind if you want to understand the news:

    1. Read a metropolitan morning newspaper for

straight news. It gives you a more complete and better organized coverage than an evening paper. If you can get a copy of *The New York Times* the day it is published, subscribe to it. If not, see if some paper in your part of the country uses *The New York Times* news service. If you live within range of the *Chicago Daily News* or if you can get a paper that subscribes to its foreign service, try to follow that, too. It is published in the evening. A list of newspapers using these two services appears in the appendix. In any case, read a newspaper that subscribes to at least two of the three press-association services—Associated Press, United Press, and International News Service.

2. Read an evening paper for its columnists, feature writers, and special correspondents. The Scripps-Howard chain has an excellent assortment, and all the newspapers belonging to this chain are also listed in the appendix. But do not tax your nerves and emotions reading columnists with whom you strongly disagree. Indulge your prejudices and read as you please.

3. Begin by reading only the headlines and remember that their purpose is not so much to describe the story underneath as it is to attract attention and thus sell papers. If the headline interests you, let your eye skim rather quickly down the column of type below. There is no quick, easy way to learn this knack except to keep at it. But if you know what you are looking for, that helps a lot.

4. The most reliable war news appears in the official communiqués, issued by the two belligerents. These com-

muniqués seldom tell the whole truth, and the side that is winning generally tells more of the truth than the loser. But the official communiqués are more reliable than the news releases from the Propaganda Ministries and the Information Bureaus of the belligerents. The trouble is that they are written in a technical style and assume more knowledge than most of us possess. This is where the military expert comes in handy. He can often interpret news better than correspondents writing on the spot and subject to censorship. As in the case of the columnists, choose the one you like best yourself.

5. If you live out of range of a metropolitan newspaper or do not want to follow the news day by day, two excellent news magazines will keep you posted. *Time* has the more complete coverage. *Newsweek* is less biased in behalf of immediate American entry into the war. You are likely to find *Life* easier to read than either and it makes better supplementary reading to a daily paper because it pictorializes and amplifies the news.

6. Do not listen to newscasters or radio news bulletins unless you are out of range of a newspaper or feel you must keep posted from hour to hour on the course of events. Newscasters give you exactly the same news you get a little later and in much more detail in your newspaper. They also take longer to speak their piece than it takes you to read it. But if you want condensed news on the radio, tune in to Elmer Davis.

7. One radio news commentator should more than

satisfy the normal appetite for news interpretation. Again, let your own preferences be your guide. But if you don't like commentators, pass them up. You will not be missing much.

8. Radio's greatest contribution to news coverage is the roundup of foreign and national news which frequently includes items you will not find in the papers. The Columbia Broadcasting System has developed this form of news coverage to a higher point than any of the other networks.

9. Specialize. Make a hobby of some one country, some one subject, some one situation. Pick out several favorite columnists and correspondents and read them regularly. In the case of news from abroad, this method is about the only way you can get around the censor.

10. Propaganda is anything you read or hear that makes you feel somebody ought to start doing something. Propaganda may be true; it may be false. The only test of propaganda is whether it works. To detect effective propaganda, watch your blood pressure and emotions. When you are getting all wrought up, the propaganda is taking hold. The point is not to resist the propaganda. The point is to recognize it.

11. More than half the exclusive, inside, confidential information you read in the newspapers or hear over the radio is false. It stands to reason that experienced reporters and news agencies are not being scooped day after day by gossip merchants, rumor artists, and purveyors of inside

stuff. And by the same token, if somebody has some really exclusive information to reveal, the chances are that the information will be released through the usual channels.

12. To recognize the reality of your own prejudices is the beginning of wisdom. Once you know what you like and dislike, begin to organize it. This means you should avoid reading or listening to news that bores you. It does not mean that you should listen to only one side of every question; it means that you should try to develop some point of view of your own. There is so much chaos in the world around you that the least you can do is to start establishing order at home.

Most books by Americans published in 1940 and dealing with world affairs end with a plea for democracy. I shall not deviate from the pattern, but, in the nature of the case, my special pleading for democracy has little to do with abstract considerations. I have tried to make this a practical book; if I am to enter a plea for democracy, it must therefore be a practical appeal.

There isn't an articulate American who has not announced his willingness to die for the principle of free speech and a free press. Without our free institutions, life would not be worth living—we all agree on that. But while it is easy to die for your principles, it is much more difficult to live up to them from day to day. In any crisis, most Americans will gladly do their duty, and more than their duty. The immediate problem, however, is not how we shall meet the crisis. The immediate problem is to prepare ourselves for the crisis when it comes.

No other country has a press as free as ours. No other country permits such freedom on the air. No other country enjoys so much free speech. And our newspaper publishers and magazine editors, our correspondents and commentators, our columnists and special writers, our radio executives and government officials, work together pretty smoothly and pretty freely. They have their shortcomings, of course, but by and large they succeed in giving us the best news coverage and the most varied news interpretation available to any people on earth. This state of affairs may not last forever, and one reason it may not last is that we have not known how to take advantage of it while we could. But exhortation does no good at all. We shall make the effort to understand the news only if that effort proves rewarding. If it does not, we shall deserve whatever comes our way.

☆ EXHIBIT D ☆

THIS IS ON ME

☆ ☆ ☆ ☆ ☆

HAVING LAID DOWN the rules for a technique of news interpretation, the least I can do is to show how they work. I shall therefore devote this closing section of the book to applying the twelve principles set forth in the last chapter. The other Exhibits have satirized other peoples' styles; here I shall not satirize my own; instead, I shall offer a case history of news interpretation.

And this is the way I shall go about it. I am writing these words on Saturday, September 28, 1940, and they will go to the printer on Monday, September 30. On Tuesday, October 1, I shall gather together the same raw material of the news that I have described elsewhere and then apply my twelve principles of news interpretation to it. The material in question will include only what the newspapers and radio programs of that one day carry. Here and there I may also refer to a current magazine article or to a book. And the interpretation will not go far beyond the events of that one day. I shall not attempt a basic analysis of the whole world situation; I shall merely apply a certain technique to twenty-four hours of world history.

If subsequent events make mincemeat of my analysis, that does not necessarily mean that the method is faulty. All it may mean is that I do not know how to adopt my own counsels of perfection. And if my analysis does fall apart, then this section of the book will at once make me look a lot more ridiculous than my own parodies have made anyone else look. Which will serve me right.

No method of analysis is any better than the person who applies it. That is why my twelfth and last principle to which I devoted the entire second chapter of the book is more important than all the rest put together. It is also the one principle that cannot be mechanically acquired or applied. I refer to the principle which emphasizes the importance of having some point of view of your own, and to illustrate that principle—not to preach my own gospel—let me list some of the guiding ideas that I myself follow in analyzing the news. I repeat: these ideas may be true or false; that is not the point here. The point here is to set up some body of ideas, some philosophy, some general point of view, to bring it to bear on current news and opinion, and to cling to it only as long as it makes sense and yields satisfaction. I therefore put forward the following general ideas, not as final truths but as working hypotheses that have stood me, at any rate, in good stead. Needless to say, they do not cover every possible contingency and all of them are subject to change without notice. But here they are:

1. I am one of those who regards the present war in

Europe as primarily a social revolution. The last European war began as a struggle for power between rival empires; it ended with revolution sweeping Russia, and all of Eastern Europe on the brink of Communism. This war began where the last one left off. Social revolution is again on the march in Germany and Eastern Europe. The Hitler movement has many revolutionary attributes, but it is also in other senses a reversion to the barbaric past. The opponents of Hitler have fought back successfully only when they have adopted methods more revolutionary than his own. By conscripting labor and wealth as well as man power, the British have moved in the same direction as the Germans; by preserving democracy and allowing labor leaders to play a bigger part in the whole scheme of things, the British have moved even farther in a revolutionary direction under Churchill than the Germans have under Hitler. In other words, the war is not a struggle between Hitler's National Socialist revolution and the supporters of the *status quo* throughout the world. It began that way and remained that kind of war until the Churchill Cabinet replaced the Chamberlain Cabinet. But it was not until the Churchill Cabinet revolutionized the British war effort that all the revolutionary implications of the struggle revealed themselves.

2. The British Empire and the British caste system that has ruled that Empire are doomed. Although Hitler may yet lose the war, the Tory aristocrats who formerly controlled the British Isles and the overseas Empire have al-

ready lost it. Some individuals may, of course, adjust themselves to the new order as Churchill quickly adjusted himself the moment he took command. But the England and the Empire the world has known for the past two centuries are gone forever.

3. The policy of the Soviet Union is wholly dictated by weakness and fear—nothing else. Stalin has no long-range understanding with Hitler. Neither is Stalin biding his time to stab Hitler in the back. The possibility that all the nations will fight until they are as weak as Russia is so remote that Stalin can hardly look forward to the prospect of revolutionizing and Communizing a bankrupt world. Rather is Stalin exclusively preoccupied with keeping the war away from Russia and thus keeping Russia out of the war. Stalin dreads above everything else a major clash with a major power. He distrusts them all equally. The Soviet Union is weak because it is a backward country which has not yet successfully organized itself on a socialistic basis. The Soviet Union is afraid because its leaders carry in their blood and bones the conviction that all the other nations plan someday and somehow to encircle and attack the first workers' state. Yet someday and somehow Stalin can hardly avoid committing himself either to Hitler or to Hitler's enemies.

4. No matter what the outcome of the fighting may be, Britain and France can never again dominate Eastern Europe and the Balkans. Although Prussia may not dominate Eastern Europe, some Austrian or Germanic federation

will make a balanced economy of Germany's industrial centers and the agricultural regions to the east and south. It is possible that all of Europe will federate as a result of the war; it is almost certain that the nations of Eastern Europe will again combine economically, as they did under the Austro-Hungarian Empire, and that Germany's industrial superiority will assert itself. As a corollary to this proposition, it seems to me almost axiomatic that the smaller nations of Europe now under German control will never regain the same kind of independence they enjoyed before the present war. The only question is whether Germany will dominate them or whether some other Continental combination will take over. My belief in the revolutionary character of the present war leads me to anticipate that the most revolutionary program will win out. And that—as I have indicated before—is not necessarily the Hitler program by any means.

5. Italy is a second-rate power trying to act like a major power. Japan is a major power trying to act like a world power. This means that Italy can never pursue a completely independent policy. Whatever decisions Mussolini himself may make can always be overruled by some major power—by an ally if not by an enemy. Not only is Italy a poor and backward country; its geographical position, its limited area and resources, and its density of population will forever prevent it from playing a great role of its own in world affairs. Japan, on the other hand, enjoys real freedom of action and can make and pursue policies without

having to take orders all along the line from larger powers. What Japan cannot do, however, is to become a world power in the sense that Britain and Germany are world powers, adopting and carrying through policies on a world-wide stage. And the reason Japan can never become a world power is that Japan does not possess sufficient resources, area, and population to get away with it.

6. India and China, the two most populous countries on earth, are in the process of emerging from feudal conditions and now stand more or less where Europe did in the seventeenth and eighteenth centuries. But because they find themselves living in a twentieth-century world, they are going through their industrial revolutions with a delayed kick. The period of colonial exploitation is over. The period of national emancipation has begun.

7. I agree with Trotsky who wrote an article in *Life*, four months before he was killed, prophesying that the United States would become the mightiest military power the world had ever seen and would take over at least a part of the British Empire—certainly Canada and possibly Australia and New Zealand. Although capitalist democracy has vanished forever from Europe, although the nineteenth-century world of free trade, the gold standard, and petty national sovereignty will never return, American capitalism has a real chance of adapting itself to changed conditions and playing a larger role than it has ever played before. Our future lies mostly but not entirely in our own hands. If we do not undertake too many commitments too

far away from home and if at the same time we reorganize ourselves internally, giving far more power to the Federal government, we have a good chance of coming out of the present war on the top of the heap and staying there for at least a generation.

Call these seven assumptions anything you like—prejudices, fixations, convictions. Go a step farther and denounce them as cockeyed nonsense. The march of events will prove or disprove most of them soon enough. All that concerns me here is to set up some frame of reference and to suggest that anyone who wants to interpret the news do likewise. Reject all my seven assumptions completely and proceed on the basis of their exact opposites. Assume if you like that this is just an old-fashioned imperialist war, that the Soviet Union is the mightiest power on earth, that the future of the British Empire lies ahead and not in the past, that Germany is done for and the smaller states of Europe will bring back to earth again the pre-Munich world. The point is to assume something and go ahead from there. But make the assumption first, because unless and until you do, you will get nowhere at all.

And now let me illustrate my twelve commandments and my seven principles:

OCTOBER 1, 1940. *Repercussions of the Triple Alliance between Germany, Italy, and Japan continue to dominate the news columns and news interpretations in the morning and evening papers. Although the alliance is now four*

224

days old, all its implications are not yet clear, and further developments are expected at any moment. Right now speculation is concentrated on the role of the Soviet Union. Any hope that the Russians would stab the Germans in the back appears doomed. The only question is whether Russia will continue to refuse further commitments in any quarter or whether a Russian-Japanese non-aggression pact is in the offing.

Louis P. Lochner, head of the Associated Press bureau in Berlin, opened his dispatch dated September 30 and appearing in the morning paper with this statement: "Despite a Nazi press chorus shouting 'All's well with Russia,' the impression prevailed in political circles tonight that negotiations between Moscow and Berlin were taking place to define more clearly the Soviet Union's role in Axis plans for a new Europe, Asia, and Africa." This news was followed by an afternoon dispatch from the Associated Press office in Berlin quoting "a usually well-informed spokesman" as saying that Germany is lending a helping hand to bring Japan and Russia together.

At the same time, the United Press office in Moscow was allowed to send out a message stating that "an attempt to improve relations between Soviet Russia and Japan was expected today as the press emphasized Nazi statements of friendship between Berlin and Moscow." The International News Service bureau in Berlin quoted neutral and official quarters in the German capital as insisting that "sympathies of the USSR will remain on the side of the

Axis." These informants do not expect the Russians to sign an outright military agreement with Germany, Italy, and Japan, but they do anticipate benevolent neutrality from Stalin.

Thus Russia continues to lurk, half distrustfully, in the shadow of Germany. It is no love of Germany that produces this behavior; it is the product of weakness, distrust, and fear. One advantage the Nazis have enjoyed over the nations of Western Europe is that they have always fully understood the weakness of Russia. They have no exaggerated fear of Communism, but they do not hesitate to play on other peoples' fear of Communism to drive a hard bargain. For years, Hitler lulled the British and French into a sense of false security by assuring them that he was protecting them from Communism. It now looks as if he had worked the same trick on the Japanese who are also inordinately afraid of Russia. Of course, the Japanese, bogged down as they are in China, have more reason to fear Russia than the British or French ever had, but they seem to have let this fear get the better of them. That is the only explanation I can see for the willingness of the Japanese to sign an agreement with Germany and Italy, an agreement which threatens them with the possibility of war with the United States.

The North American Newspaper Alliance released a special article in the morning papers by the Japanese publicist, K. K. Kawakami, who is registered at the State Department as Washington correspondent for two big

Japanese newspapers. For years, Mr. Kawakami has been regarded as a "propagandist" for Japan in the United States because he has frequently pleaded the Japanese cause. But the alliance his country has made with Germany and Italy is too much for him. He calls it a "one-sided affair" that "benefits Germany, but puts Japan at a disadvantage." Here is the way he analyzes the alliance, "The plausible explanation is that Tokyo was scared into accepting Herr Hitler's terms by the bogey he held up of a possible Anglo-German compromise and a German-Soviet alliance, both aimed at Japan." The only real advantage Mr. Kawakami can see in the pact is a "possible easing of tension" between Japan and Russia. This consideration, however, is vastly overbalanced by the fact that from now on Japan will have to take its share of the hatred that the United States is directing against Hitler and all his works. In Japanese terms, it means that the pro-German military clique in Tokyo has routed the pro-American group with which Mr. Kawakami identifies himself.

Nevertheless, William H. Stoneman, the Chicago Daily News correspondent in London, quotes an editorial in the London Times urging the United States to appease Japan. "It is certain," writes Mr. Stoneman, "that The Times expresses the attitude of people who in the past have guided British policy." Another dispatch from another Chicago Daily News correspondent in London suggests that these same people who used to guide British policy and whose names are associated with the word "appeasement" have not entirely disappeared from responsible positions. Helen Kirkpatrick, who has excellent contacts with antiappeasement elements in Britain, reports that a rift may develop in the British Cabinet because of Lord Beaverbrook's unwillingness to co-operate with the Labor leaders, Morrison and Bevin. Beaverbrook is a maverick Conservative who has stepped up airplane production, gained the confidence of Churchill, but who is now being accused of not running the industry under his control as well as the Labor people are running the industries under their control.

What we are witnessing in England today was eloquently described in a five-minute broadcast from London by Edward R. Murrow over the Columbia Broadcasting System. "Mark it down," Mr. Murrow kept repeating, that we are living through a revolution, that we are witnessing the death of an age. He praised the courage of the British people and the liberality of their government which has allowed more pamphlets to be published during the past three weeks of bombardment than during any other period of the war. These pamphlets, Mr. Murrow continued, dwelt largely on the shortcomings of Britain's present leadership. They complained about the failure at Dakar, the lack of any program of war aims, the continuation of 800,000 men on the dole at a time when the country is fighting for its life. Mr. Murrow flatly stated that the only thing that can free France from Hitler is revolution and he added, just as flatly, that the present British government is incapable of promoting revolution anywhere, for Parliament remains overwhelmingly Conservative. Yet, as Mr. Murrow said, it reflects nothing but credit on the spirit of the present government that he was allowed to report as he did and to repeat to an audience of unnumbered millions of Americans that Europe is fighting a revolution rather than a war and that Britain needs to become more revolutionary to survive.

The military front produced a really important announcement today. The German High Command made it known, through a spokesman, that "General Hunger" would march against the British Isles this winter. At the same time, the British Admiralty admitted that Britain had lost more shipping last week than in any week since the war began. The German pronouncement means that the Germans have abandoned—or else want the world to believe they have abandoned—their plans to invade Britain this year. The British pronouncement does not mean that the Germans will succeed in their plan to concentrate on blockade rather than invasion. It does mean, however, that Britain is in for a hard winter.

Wythe Williams reported tonight on the radio that the Germans have been using young, inexperienced pilots in their bombings of Britain. He says they are saving their best men for some bigger task to come. But he wonders if the Germans are not making the same mistake they have made in other wars when they had victory in their grasp, because it looks more and more as if the Royal Air Force were carrying the war to the enemy. Moreover, the dependable Wallace Carroll of the United Press reports from London that the British air defenses have greatly improved. More and more it looks like a long-drawn-out war in which the populations on both sides will be subjected to increasing strain. Indeed, civilian morale may prove the determining factor.

Meanwhile, the United States is getting ready for trouble, too. The House of Representatives passed today and sent to the White House the excess-profits tax bill which rounds out the Administration's defense program. But if the country is united on the necessity for national defense, it is not united on the question of who should organize the defense or for what purposes the defense shall be used. William Philip Simms, foreign editor for the Scripps-Howard newspapers, echoes the appeal of his chief, Roy Howard, who has urged the United States to send a commission to Japan to work out some Far Eastern settlement. Mr. Howard has been writing a series of articles direct from the Far East, calling attention to the dangerous position the Roosevelt Administration maneuvered itself into when it slapped the scrap-iron embargo on Japan last Thursday, the day before the German-Italian-Japanese Pact was signed. Mr. Simms quoted an article by the Japanese Ambassador to Washington, Kensuke Horinouchi, expressing agreement with Mr. Howard's point of view and urging the appointment of an American commission to come to Japan. One cannot help wondering, however, whether the Japanese would be quite so eager to reach an understanding with the United States if this country had not at long last declared an embargo on scrap-iron shipments—even though the embargo does not officially take effect until October 16.

Those who want background on the whole Far Eastern situation, especially the question of a possible Japanese-American war, should consult a book published today entitled Our Future in Asia, by Robert Aura Smith. The thesis of this book is that the United States has a big stake in Asia and can defend it if it takes a firm stand, such as the Administration has taken in declaring its embargo. But there is no denying that we must pay a heavy price if we plan to play a big role in the world. Yesterday Dorothy Thompson said that the German-Italian-Japanese combination made it necessary for us to subordinate everything to national defense. She foresaw Hitler putting a lever under the whole world if we do not stop him—and immediately. Walter Lippmann made the same point in more reasoned fashion in this morning's paper, and what he has to say is all the more striking because it comes from a man of conservative views. I have seen no more courageous and realistic appraisal of what this country must do than these words of Mr. Lippmann's:

"Neither the Administration in its policy nor Mr. Willkie in his speeches seems to have grasped the fact that if we are to have total defense we cannot carry on business as usual either under the methods of the New Deal or under the methods which Mr. Willkie prefers. We cannot carry on business as usual and have total defense. We cannot eat our cake and have it too. We cannot make an omelet and not break the eggs. The British tried it until the disaster in France, maintaining business as nearly usual as possible with Mr. Chamberlain and 'social reform' as nearly usual as possible to please the Labor Party."

Mr. Willkie is presenting himself to the voters as the American equivalent of Winston Churchill. Yet Mr. Willkie has announced in the next breath that he would call in on the defense program precisely the same type of industrialist and banker who almost lost the war for Britain. David Lawrence, who supports Willkie and takes a far more conservative line than Walter Lippmann, has a column today saying Hitler would prefer to have Roosevelt rather than Willkie as President because "the fact is that Herr Hitler has outbluffed and outmaneuvered Mr. Roosevelt these last two years and is doubtless confident he can do it again." This interpretation hardly squares with the fact that Roosevelt's destroyers-for-bases deal aroused very little enthusiasm in Berlin. It is, however, a fair enough argument for Mr. Lawrence to bring forward because Roosevelt's supporters are trying to convince the country that a vote for Willkie is a vote for Hitler. The truth of the matter is that both parties in the present campaign are saying things about the other that they will be only too glad to forget and apologize for the moment the votes are in— no matter who wins.

Let me conclude by summing up the high spots in today's news. The revolutionary aspect of the present war is receiving increasing attention not only in Great Britain but right here in the United States where even conservatives are beginning to understand that "total defense" comes pretty close to being revolution itself. And it looks as if we'd be in for a long period of "total defense" because the Germans are thinking of the Battle of Britain in terms of years—not weeks. At the same time, tension is increasing in the Far East. Japan now seems to have got the short end of the stick in the recent alliance with Germany and Italy while Russia is leaning more toward the Axis than toward Britain or the United States. The British, fearful that the United States may actually go to war in the Far East, urge that we appease Japan. The same policy finds some support in this country and would no doubt be welcomed by the Japanese who cannot enjoy the position they now occupy. It seems probable, however, that the Roosevelt Administration will bide its time because overtures to Japan at this stage of the game would make the strong stand we took five days ago look like a ridiculous piece of bluff if we weaken so soon. But whether we appease or oppose Japan we are already committed, not only by our own decisions but by forces beyond our control, to play a bigger part in world affairs and to make changes in our own way of living similar to those changes going forward in the world around us.

APPENDIX

☆ ☆ ☆ ☆ ☆

In accordance with the principle of giving the reader a break I am listing here some of the news sources that I have mentioned in the course of the text. All the magazines I have referred to can be purchased at any newsstand. Radio programs are subject to occasional change and are listed anyway in the daily paper. I am therefore confining myself here to indicating where you can find certain news sources.

For instance, if you do not read *The New York Times* you can nevertheless find its news service, covering both Washington and foreign news, in the following newspapers:

Chicago Tribune
Milwaukee Journal
St. Louis Globe-Democrat
Buffalo Courier and Express
Philadelphia Record
Baltimore Sun
Washington Post
Boston Herald

Montreal Gazette
Toronto Globe and Mail

You will also find the foreign service of the *Chicago Daily News* in the following newspapers outside Chicago:

New York Post
Detroit News
Cleveland Press
Pittsburgh Press
St. Louis Post-Dispatch
Manchester (New Hampshire) Union-Leader
San Francisco Examiner
Baltimore Evening Sun
Minneapolis Star Journal
Des Moines Register
Dayton Journal Herald
Washington Star
Buffalo News
Boston Evening Transcript
Philadelphia Bulletin
Portland Oregonian
Dallas Journal
Memphis Democrat
Milwaukee Post
Ketchikan Alaska Chronicle
Winnipeg Free Press
Vancouver Daily Province

Montreal Standard
Toronto Daily Star

These newspapers belong to the Scripps-Howard chain and use most of the Scripps-Howard columnists and feature writers as well as United Press news:

New York World-Telegram
Cleveland Press
Pittsburgh Press
Cincinnati Post
Columbus Citizen
San Francisco News
Indianapolis News
Knoxville News-Sentinel
Memphis Press-Scimitar
Memphis Commercial-Appeal
Birmingham Post
Houston Press
Fort Worth Press
El Paso Herald-Post
Albuquerque Tribune
Covington Kentucky Post
Denver Rocky Mountain News
Evansville Press

William Randolph Hearst controls nineteen papers to Roy Howard's eighteen, but they are not scattered in so many cities. These papers carry the feature writers of the International News Service:

New York Journal-American
New York Mirror
Albany Times-Union
Boston Record
Boston American
Boston Sunday Advertiser
Baltimore News-Post
Baltimore Sunday American
Pittsburgh Sun-Telegraph
Chicago Herald-American
Milwaukee News-Sentinel
Detroit Times
San Francisco Examiner
San Francisco Call-Bulletin
Oakland Post-Enquirer
Los Angeles Examiner
Los Angeles Herald-Express
San Antonio Light
Seattle Post-Intelligencer

Here are some of the leading news letters, with prices and addresses:

KIPLINGER WASHINGTON LETTER. National Press Bldg., Washington, D. C. Weekly. $18 a year.

WHALEY-EATON SERVICE. Munsey Bldg., Washington, D. C. Weekly. American letter $25 a year. Foreign letter $30 a year.

BUSINESS AND LEGISLATION REPORT. The Research Institute of America, 292 Madison Avenue, New York City. Weekly. $20 a year.

INTERNATIONAL STATISTICAL BUREAU FOREIGN LETTER. 70 Fifth Avenue, New York City. Fortnightly. $7.50 for six months.

UNCENSORED. 112 East 19 St., New York City. Weekly. $2.50 for six months.

WEEK BY WEEK. 3034 P St., N.W. Washington, D. C. Weekly. $5 a year.

IN FACT. Chatham-Phenix Building, Long Island City, N. Y. Fortnightly. 22 issues for 25 cents.

The following recent books continue to throw light on world news:

POWERFUL AMERICA, by Eugene J. Young. Stokes, 1937. $3.00. The former cable editor of *The New York Times* outlines an imperial policy for America.

UNTO CAESAR, by F. A. Voigt. Putnam, 1938. $2.50. A former *Manchester Guardian* correspondent draws some original parallels between Fascism and Communism.

THE END OF ECONOMIC MAN, by Peter F. Drucker. John Day, 1939. $2.50. An Austrian economist and journalist anticipates the Nazi-Soviet Pact, outlines Hitler's policy of eastward expansion, and probes the philosophic roots of Fascism.

STALIN, by Boris Souvarine. Alliance Book Corporation, 1939. $3.75. The most comprehensive book about the Russian dictator in any language.

THE FAR EASTERN POLICY OF THE UNITED STATES, by A. Whitney Griswold. Harcourt, Brace, 1939. $3.75. A masterly survey of Far Eastern affairs during the past forty years with special reference to the United States.

AMERICAN WHITE PAPER, by Joseph Alsop and Robert Kintner. Simon and Schuster, 1940. $1.00. The closest approximation to an authoritative account of American foreign policy from Munich to the fall of France.

THE DYNAMICS OF WAR AND REVOLUTION, by Lawrence Dennis. The Weekly Foreign Letter, 1940. $3.00. An American Fascist's cynical analysis of the world situation. Required reading for liberals only.

THE STRATEGY OF TERROR, by Edmond Taylor. Houghton Mifflin, 1940. $2.50. How Hitler's propaganda helped to bring about the fall of France. The author is an American newspaperman who remained in France until after the defeat.

MEIN KAMPF, by Adolf Hitler. Reynal and Hitchcock, 1939. $3.00. Although Hitler has not followed this schedule to the letter, it remains the most authoritative book about Nazi Germany.

OUR FUTURE IN ASIA, by Robert Aura Smith. Viking Press, 1940. $3.00. The case for American intervention in the Far East.

INDEX

☆ ☆ ☆   ☆ ☆

241

ABOUT THE AUTHOR

☆ ☆ ☆ ☆ ☆

Since his graduation from Harvard in 1921, Quincy Howe has devoted a large part of his time to the study of world affairs. On leaving Harvard he spent a year of travel and study abroad, returning to work for the next six years with the Atlantic Monthly Company. Most of his duties were concentrated on The Living Age, and in 1929 he followed the magazine to New York to become its editor for another six years. His first book, World Diary: 1929–1934, appeared in 1934. In 1935 he became head of the editorial department at Simon and Schuster. In 1937 he wrote England Expects Every American to Do His Duty and in 1939 Blood Is Cheaper Than Water: The Prudent American's Guide to Peace and War. In August, 1939, he began commenting on world news for Station WQXR in New York and now speaks from that station three times a week. He is married and is the father of two children.